ZEN AND THE COMIC SPIRIT.

Conrad Hyers

THE WESTMINSTER PRESS
PHILADELPHIA

© M. Conrad Hyers 1973

Published by The Westminster Press ®
Philadelphia, Pennsylvania

Printed in the United States of America

Library of Congress Cataloging in Publication Data

Hyers, M. Conrad.
  Zen and the comic spirit.

  Includes bibliographical references.
  1. Zen Buddhism and humor. I. Title.
BQ4570.H85H9 1974   294.3'927   74–628
ISBN 0–664–20705–7
ISBN 0–664–24989–2 (pbk.)

For Gerry

ZEN AND THE COMIC SPIRIT

BOOKS BY CONRAD HYERS

Published by The Westminster Press

Zen and the Comic Spirit

The Chickadees

ZEN AND THE COMIC SPIRIT

Self-portrait in the image of Pu-tai   HAKUIN

Contents

Illustrations

Acknowledgements

I should like to express my appreciation for a Ford Foundation Asian Studies Grant, enabling me to participate in a faculty conference on Buddhism in the summer of 1968 where the fledgling outlines of this book were hesitantly advanced, and where I profited from the reservations, doubts and encouragements of the colleagues of that experience, especially Joseph Kitagawa, Winston King, Bardwell Smith, Walpole Rahula, David Yu, Frank Reynolds, Lewis Williams and Frank Wong. Appreciation is also due for another Non-Western Studies Fellowship from the Ford Foundation which supported a term of research and writing at the University of Hawaii and the East-West Center, in the winter of 1970; for a Younger Humanist Fellowship from the National Endowment for the Humanities which provided the sabbatical time in 1970–1 for further development of the manuscript; and for a fellowship from the Fund for the Study of the Great Religions which afforded the opportunity of study and dialogue in Asia in the autumn of 1971.

Special acknowledgement must be given to Eliot Deutsch in whom the preliminary essay of the project struck a responsive chord, and to *Philosophy East and West*, of which he is the editor, for publishing it under the title, 'The Ancient Zen Master as Clown-Figure and Comic Midwife' (January, 1970). Similar acknowledgement is due Masao Abe, and the editorial board of *The Eastern Buddhist* of which he is a member, for encouraging the publication of the materials of Chapter Three in the May, 1972, issue of that journal under the title, 'The Comic Perspective in Zen Literature and Art.' Derek Southall, editor of *The Middle Way*, has likewise given his encouragement by offering portions of Chapter Four in the May and

August, 1972, issues of that periodical under the titles' 'Zen and the Commonplace' and 'Zen and the Comic Acceptance of the Absurd.'

I am also indebted to Christmas Humphreys of the London Buddhist Society, Ben Kimpel of Drew University, Thomas Berry of Fordham University, and Joseph Campbell, formerly of Sarah Lawrence College, whose kind letters of enthusiasm and suggestion provided welcome inspiration at critical junctures of the writing. Gratitude must go, too, to the various Zen masters and Buddhist scholars who gave me the benefit of their reactions and criticisms during my stay in Japan, particularly Nanrei Kobori, Sohaku Ogata, Eshin Nishimura, Shojun Bando and Masao Abe. And a very special appreciation is to be given to the Sōtō monks of Sōji-ji monastery who permitted the opportunity of sharing in their common life.

I should also like to give due recognition to my children, Jon, Dean and Lauri, whose innocent playfulness and laughter have frequently interrupted these labours with a nostalgic reminder of the 'little Zen' of the child, and a foretaste of the 'foolishness' of the sage. For it is, in part, in relation to those childlike experiences of wonder and acceptance, of carefree immediacy and spontaneous delight, that these essays stand as a kind of remembrance, a recollection and a return on a higher level no doubt, but to those truths which are always and everywhere known, yet so easily forgotten and ignored.

> *Your singing-and-dancing is none other than*
> *the voice of Dharma.*
>   *Zazen Wasan*, Hakuin

The author wishes to thank the publishers who have given permission to use material from their publications as indicated in the 'Notes' to chapters and also to the following:

Edmund R. Brill, *The Basic Writings of Sigmund Freud,* translated and edited by A. A. Brill, © 1938 by Random House Inc.; renewed © 1965 by Gioia B. Bernheim and Edmund R. Brill. Reprinted by permission.

Doubleday and Company Inc.: *An Introduction to Haiku* by Harold G. Henderson, © 1958. Reprinted by permission.

Zen: Poems, Prayers, Sermons, Anecdotes, Interviews by Lucien Stryk and Takashi Ikemoto, © 1963, 1965. Reprinted by permission.

Faber and Faber Ltd: *Sengai, The Zen Master* by D. T. Suzuki, © 1971 by the Matsugaoka Bunko Foundation. Plates 34 and 40 and quotations used by permission of Faber and Faber Ltd and the Matsugaoka Bunko Foundation.

A History of Zen Buddhism by Heinrich Dumoulin, S.J., translated by Paul Peachey, © 1963. Reprinted by permission of Faber and Faber Ltd and Random House Inc.

Grove Press Inc.: *Manual of Zen Buddhism* by D. T. Suzuki. Plate XI and text used by permission of Grove Press Inc. and Hutchinson and Co. Ltd, all rights reserved.

Harcourt Brace Jovanovich Inc.: *The Zen Koan* by Miura and Sasaki, © 1965 by Ruth Fuller Sasaki. Plate I and calligraphy reprinted by permission of Harcourt Brace Jovanovich Inc.

Cricket Songs: Japanese Haiku, translated by Harry Behn, © 1964. Haiku by Masahide on page 167 reprinted by permission of Harcourt Brace Jovanovich Inc.

Hokuseido Press: *Oriental Humour* by R. H. Blyth, © 1959.

Zen and Zen Classics by R. H. Blyth, Volumes II, IV and V, © 1969–70.

National Council of Churches of Christ: From The Revised Standard Version Bible, used by permission.

New Directions Publishing Corporation: Buddha, *The Dhammapada* translated by Irving Babbitt, © 1936 by Edward S. Babbitt and Esther B. Howe. Reprinted by permission of the New Directions Publishing Corporation and Laurence P. Pollinger, Ltd.

Pantheon Books—A Division of Random House Inc.: *Original Teachings of Ch'an Buddhism* by Chang Chung-yuan, © 1969. Used by permission of the publisher.

The Way of Zen by Alan W. Watts, © 1957. Used by permission of the publisher.

The World of Zen, edited by Nancy Wilson Ross, © 1960. Used by permission of the publisher.

Princeton University Press: *Hero with A Thousand Faces,* Joseph Campbell, Bollingen Series XVII, © 1949 by the Bollingen Foundation. Reprinted by permission of Princeton University Press.

Philosophical Fragments by Søren Kierkegaard, translated by David F. Swenson, © 1936. Revised edition, with a new introduction and commentary by Niels Thulstrup; translation revised and commentary translated by Howard V. Hong, © 1962. Reprinted by permission of Princeton University Press.

Principles of Chinese Painting, second impression, by George Rowley, © 1959. Reprinted by permission of Princeton University Press.

Zen and Japanese Culture, D. T. Suzuki, © 1959 by Bollingen Foundation. Plate 6 and poetry reprinted by permission of Princeton University Press.

The Ronald Press Company: *Chinese Painting, Leading Masters and Principles* in seven volumes by Osvald Siren, volumes I, II, IV and V, © 1956 and 1958. Used by permission of The Ronald Press Company and Percy Lund Humphries and Company Ltd.

St John's University Press: *The Platform Sutra,* translated by Wing-Tsit Chan, Asian Institute Translation number 3, © 1963.

The Tao Teh Ching of Lao Tzu, translated by John C. H. Wu, Asian Institute Translation 1, © 1961.

Charles E. Tuttle Inc.: *The Iron Flute* by N. Senzaki and Ruth McCandless, © 1961.

Zen and Oriental Art by Hugo Munsterberg, © 1965, Plates 4, 5 and 24 and quotations reprinted by permission.

Zen Flesh and Zen Bones by Paul Reps and Nyogen Senzaki, © 1957.

Viking Press Inc.: *The Masks of God: Primitive Mythology* by Joseph Campbell, © 1969. Reprinted by permission.

Acknowledgement is also gratefully given to the following for permission to use reproductions of original paintings and sketches: Benrido Company, Kyoto, for a scene from *Chōjū-Giga.*

Eisei Bunko Foundation, Tokyo, for two 'Self-portraits' by Hakuin, from the Marquis Moritatsu Collection.

Idemitsu Art Gallery, Tokyo, for 'Tanha Burning the Buddha Image' and 'The Meditating Frog' by Sengai, from the Sazo Idemitsu Collection.

Kosetsu Museum of Art, Kobe, for the 'Dancing Pu-tai' by Liang-k'ai from the Murayama Collection.

Mr Takanaru Mitsui for 'Hui-nēng Tearing up the Sutras' by Liang-k'ai, from his private collection.

Boston Museum of Fine Arts, for 'The Three Laughing Monks at Hu-Hsi' by Soga Shōhaku (right fold of a two-fold screen).

Shōkokuji, Kyoto, for the 'Tenth Cow-herding Picture' by Shubun.

Tokyo National Museum for 'Han-shan and Shih-tē' by Yen-hui.

I regret that I have been unable to locate the present owner of 'Bodhidharma' by Matabei, originally housed in the T. Takeoka Collection.

Preface

A million Mount Sumerus are but a drop of dew
  On the end of a single hair;
Three thousand worlds are only a seagull
  Floating on the ocean waves.
The two children of the tiny creatures
  In the eyebrow of a mosquito
Never stop quarrelling between themselves
  As to whose earth this is.
HAKUIN[1]

In writing a book about Zen one has the double sensation of attempting, on the one hand, to compress a million Mount Sumerus into the tip of a single hair, and, on the other hand, to inflate the utter simplicity of a single hair into a million Mount Sumerus. One also has the haunting suspicion that one is turning into an argument, a debate, perhaps even a quarrel, what is only available as a fundamental intuition and experience which no amount of discussion in itself can effect, and which may simply result in a dispute as to who possesses authentic title to what is freely open to all.

On how to sing
  The frog school and the skylark school
  Are arguing.

Shiki[2]

The radically intuitive, experiential and 'wordless' character of Zen (not to mention the comic spirit) does not easily lend itself to book form, as anyone who has entertained the notion of writing about Zen, or the prospect of being taken for an 'authority' on the 'subject,' is inevitably aware. There is a certain humour in the very suggestion of offering a book on Zen, let alone on Zen and humour, which is not unlike pro-positioning a man with a fish and giving him a stone – or an embalmed cat! Any addition, accordingly, to the already long parade of books which Zen has elicited in recent decades – no matter how neglected and important its theme, or how unique and intriguing its approach – must be willing to be placed, from the start, within the comic parenthesis of master Chao-chou's exclamation on joining the funeral procession for one of his monks: 'What a long train of dead bodies follows in the wake of a single living person!'[3]

Yet hopefully, despite these and other limitations, the reception will be more favourable than that which Bodhid-harma, the first patriarch of Chinese Zen (Ch'an), is alleged to have given to one of the Chinese classics when brought before him in order to solicit his reaction to its significance. Taking the book, he put it to his nose: 'It has a kind of quarrelsome smell about it!'[4]

The Oddity of Zen

There are many ways into the way of Zen. Essays and books have been written on Zen in its relationship to art, archery, the tea ceremony, the martial arts, *haiku* poetry, the *Noh* theatre, gardening, flower arrangement, and even cookery. But of these various ways, or even of the ways added by foreign and largely alien interests in psychoanalysis, comparative philosophy and religion, to approach Zen from the standpoint of its relationship to the comic spirit will no doubt appear to be, at first sight, the oddest and most oblique – as well as the most likely to stir a controversy between the skylark school and the frog school!

On the one hand this reaction is entirely fitting, considering the place of the odd, the eccentric and the outlandish in humour, clowning and comedy as part of their very point and play. This *is* the odd way into Zen. But it is also the odd way of Zen itself, and an important part of the oft-noted 'oddity' of Zen. It is, therefore, not nearly so odd in relation to Zen as it might appear to be in relation to any other religious tradi-tion, whether within or without the Buddhist world. Where else could one meet a stranger assortment of spiritual guides, teaching methods and religious expressions? In no other tradition could the entire 'syndrome' of laughter, humour, comedy and 'clowning' be said to be more visible and pronounced than in Zen, where the comic spirit has been duly rescued from those miscellaneous and peripheral moments to which it is so commonly assigned and restricted. So much is this so that it is difficult to imagine authentic Zen, or to survey the unusual history of Zen, completely apart from the comic vision.

As remarkable and unique as this is, however, it is the one dimension of Zen that has been given the least appreciation and interpretation. To be sure, references to the prominence and importance of comic elements in Zen and Zen art are scattered through much of the literature on Zen. And two brief essays have been devoted to it in English by R. H. Blyth and D. T. Suzuki.[5] The significance of this, nonetheless, far exceeds the meagre attention it has received. In no other religious movement are its principal records (comprised largely of anecdotes relating to the lives and sayings of masters), its techniques for spiritual realisation, its art and aesthetic, and its portrayals of the spirit and style of those masters whom one is called to emulate, so intimately intertwined with the comic spirit and perspective.

It is not easy to identify the reasons for the neglect of this 'other side' of Zen, except to attribute it to the widespread taboo against associating the comic too closely with the sacred. Comic elements of whatever sort, found in connection with religious forms, we are often inclined, at best, to relegate to some presumably minor and inferior category – something on the order of an embellishment, like spice added to rice, which may give a certain palatability to religion at the elementary level, or a reprieve from its rigours, but is not an essential ingredient, and decidedly not the stuff of the religious life itself. At worst, we are inclined to see the comic as a distraction from, if not an eventual negation of, the seriousness and earnestness and holiness of the religious task – to be moving away from rather than toward religious goals and spiritual attainments. As a result, in most traditions outside of Zen, the various protagonists of the comic – whether iconoclast, humourist, clown or fool – have been barred from the temple precincts, and kept strolling in the streets, or imprisoned under ecclesiastical interdicts.

Such prejudices, often shared by priest and scholar alike, belie a failure to understand the importance, in fact necessity, of the interplay between the sacred and the comic. Much too hastily is it presupposed that the comic is either so trivial that it has nothing to say, or that it is so pointed in what it has to say that it is threatening and destructive. Yet the comic spirit and perspective plays a far greater and more significant role in religious experience and expression than priestly safekeeping and scholarly investigation have been ready to admit or careful to recognise. Nowhere is this more evident, or more profoundly appreciated, than in the case of Zen.

Running Sideways

Important as calling attention to this may be, nevertheless to write a book about Zen and the comic spirit demands a measure of hesitancy because of the understandable frustration and dismay, if not justifiable 'holy indignation,' of Zennists over Western books on Zen. For Western Zen and Western interpretations of Zen often reflect more talent in revealing the nature of Westernisation than that of Zen. It is not that Westerners are singularly impervious to and incapable of Zen, but that the cultural and religious background of the West commonly moves in such different and even alien directions that so often Zen is appropriated for the wrong reasons, fostered by half-correct or simply incorrect expectations and interpretations. As Nyogen Senzaki protested with respect to the Americanisation of Zen: '[It] is running sideways writing books, lecturing, referring to theology, psychology, and what not. Someone should stand up and smash the whole thing to pieces . . .'[6] This kind of 'smashing,' however, is itself characteristic of the iconoclastic temper of Zen – and of the comic as well – and is an important part of the comic method and vision of Zen.

The present effort is no doubt a form of 'running sideways' in pointing toward and appreciating these dimensions of Zen. Yet, like the man who runs back and forth along the river bank calling attention to the fact that it is actually possible to cross over to the other shore, there may be some value, however limited and provisional, in moving sideways in order to move forward. Just as surely, though, the fool is one who confuses a great expenditure of energy in running back and forth with the accomplishment of actually getting somewhere. From the Zen standpoint such a person is not a little like the small boy who shifts nervously from one foot to the other, while the real problem is that he needs to go and find a lavatory. One master, indeed, is reputed to have replied, in answer to a monk's inquiry as to the present abode of the Buddha: 'The Buddha is in the outhouse!' Once man has realised the comedy in his situation he is already on his way to Zen, which is itself an illustration of one of the many affiliations between Zen and the comic spirit.

Still there is a certain precariousness in writing about the comic spirit, as well as the Zen spirit, in any context. For as with all things in the realm of the spirit, to talk too long, to examine too meticulously, to pile qualification upon qualification and add theory to theory, is to be in danger of upsetting the delicate balance of that life which one wishes to understand, or of destroying the fragile tissue into which one wishes to breathe new life. Here, too, 'the letter kills, while only the spirit gives life.' The book, therefore, is intentionally short, and no doubt omits many of those niceties of notation and delimitation which might enable the operation to be more successful at the expense of killing the patient.

The book is not, of course, nearly as short as might exemplify Zen, which might well be more accurately illustrated simply by offering a few humorous *kōans* and anecdotes, and concluding with an abrupt '*Kwatz!*' Yet in a context which is not steeped in Buddhism or Oriental culture this has never been sufficient, and opens itself to too many misuses and misinterpretations. There is therefore a place for restrained interpretation; while at the same time it must be undertaken only from within a keen awareness of the comic awkwardness about the very proposal to analyse both Zen and the comic spirit. For analysis has a way of failing to participate in the very spirit which it would analyse, and therefore not only involving itself in an ironic self-contradiction, but in a violation and negation of that to which it is attempting to do justice.

Recognising the awkwardness of this dilemma, the effort has been made, as far as the stubborn woodenness of language and the sterility of verbal interpretation will permit, not only to point to but enter into the spirit of Zen, and the *comic* spirit of Zen. From an academic standpoint this is a spirit and a perspective that must be defined, and defined with all due philosophical and psychological precision. Yet from a Zen standpoint it must, above all, be experienced, while academic definitions have a special facility for standing squarely in the way of such experience and its understanding from within that experience. Such, in fact, is the concern of many a Zen anecdote. Master Chao-chou, for example, was once asked, 'When the entire body decomposes, something spiritual seems to remain. What becomes of it?' As the monk awaited a disquisition which would clarify the doctrine, Chao-chou replied, 'The wind is blowing again this morning!'[7]

It must be emphasised, then, that though there are many ways into the way of Zen, along with which the present approach may be classified, in the final sense there are *no* ways, as if it were simply a matter of proceeding down a certain established path, or discovering some magic key that might unlock Wu-mēn's celebrated 'gateless gate to Zen experience.' All ways into Zen are limited by the peculiarity that they never arrive at their destination, like an endless guided tour around the outside walls of one monastery after another. The pointing finger, however straight and accurate, never quite reaches the moon!

Fixing and Not Fixing the Standards
A wide range of terms have been introduced in an effort to

point in the direction of this 'other side' of Zen – terms which are loosely related, and in some of their forms not necessarily related, or simply not related at all: smiling, laughing, joking, clowning, as well as nonsense, humour, comedy, absurdity, foolishness and playfulness. Obviously the concern here is not with any kind of smiling, laughing, joking and clowning, or with any kind of context in which these expressions may occur. Laughter may be sadistic, demented, nervous, morbid, crude, teasing, taunting, cynical, bitter. Humour may be a way of evading truth and avoiding responsibility. Joking may be a convenient vehicle for ridiculing others in order to magnify one's own ego and fortify one's own prejudices. Comedy may contain expressions of hostility and aggression, fear and anxiety, and so forth. Certainly, therefore, laughter, smiling and joking are not necessarily reliable indices of the comic spirit, nor are all kinds of nonsense, absurdity and playfulness necessarily informed by the comic perspective.

It is to be acknowledged, in fact, that in putting together such a broad spectrum of terms and phenomena, albeit related, and however qualified, the result may be seen as guilty of the exhaustively conglomerate definition which Corbyn Morris in his *Essay Towards Fixing the True Standards of Wit, Humour, Raillery, Satire, and Ridicule* (1744), saw as the principal success and failure of Dr. Barrow's *Sermon Against Foolish Talking and Jesting*:

> There being perhaps no variety, in all the extent of these subjects, which he has not presented to view in (his) description ... For instead of exhibiting the properties of wit in a clearer light, and confuting the false claims which are made to it, he has made it his whole business to perplex it the more by introducing, from all corners, a monstrous troop of new and unexpected pretenders!

Such terms, nevertheless, serve to point in the direction of that 'other side' of existence, and of the human spirit, which is only too commonly seen as *outside*, if not inimical to, religious concerns and spiritual attainments. In relation to the ultra-seriousness and anxiety, and consequently the fanaticism and dogmatism, which frequently accompany the intensities of religious conviction and commitment, this definitely contains an element of truth. For what unites all these 'lighter' manifestations of the spirit is a lightheartedness and playfulness which refuses to absolutise, or to take with an inflexible and unqualified seriousness, anything – especially one's self and one's situation. In its highest Zen form, it is the refusal, born of the freedom and perspective which in Buddhism is known as enlightenment, to be contained within and defined by the vicious circle of grasping and clinging, and that resists the temptation to enter the bondage of attachment to anything, however consequential or sacred. And at this point the 'other side' of the comic and the 'this side' of seriousness and sacrality become one in the freedom of him who has gone beyond holy and unholy, sense and nonsense, having and not-having, self and other.

In stating the matter in this way, it is clear that we have to do here with a very special kind of spirit and perspective, which it will be the task of the following essays to attempt to delineate as it is developed in Zen Buddhism. It is a spirit and perspective, an outlook upon life and a way of life, which involves a very special stance and set of attitudes in relation to existence. It is a way of perceiving reality and of experiencing reality, of being real, and not just any parlour witticism, clownish caper, or comedian's trick that commands our attention.

Beloit College   M. CONRAD HYERS

Notes

1. R. H. Blyth, *Zen and Zen Classics*, 7 volumes (Tokyo: Hokuseido, 1960–70), V, page 198.
2. Harold G. Henderson, *An Introduction to Haiku* (Garden City: Doubleday, 1958), page 169.
3. John C. H. Wu, *The Golden Age of Zen* (Taipei: National War College, 1967), page 145.

4. Chiang Yee, *The Chinese Eye*, 2nd edition (London: Norton, 1936), page 81.

5. R. H. Blyth, *Oriental Humour* (Tokyo: Hokuseido, 1959), pages 87–97. Daisetz T. Suzuki, *Sengai, the Zen Master* (New York: New York Graphic Society, 1971), pages 1–17.

6. Nyogen Senzaki and Ruth S. McCandless, trans. with commentary of Genro's 'Solid Iron Flute,' *The Iron Flute* (Rutland: Tuttle, 1961), page 126.

7. Heinrich Dumoulin, *A History of Zen Buddhism* (New York: Random House, 1963), page 100.

The Dragon's Song

Monk: 'What is Tao?'
Ts'ao-shan: 'A dragon singing in the dry wood.'
Monk: 'I wonder whether there is anyone who can hear this?'
Ts'ao-shan: 'There is no one in the entire world who does not hear this.'
Monk: 'I do not know what kind of composition the dragon's song is.'
Ts'ao-shan: 'I also do not know; but all who hear it lose themselves.'

The Transmission of the Lamp

ONE   *The Smile of Truth*

When one has understanding, one should laugh;
   One should not weep.
HSÜEH-T'OU

The smile of Asian peoples has often been represented, usually in the caricatures of politically inspired cartooning and the stereotypes of popular Caucasian imagination, to which both the Chinese and Japanese have been subjected. But that smile, insofar as it corresponds to reality at all, has a profound basis in the unusual stress in both Chinese and Japanese culture upon the human sphere and the natural graces, and indeed upon the most practical, earthen, everyday phenomena of life. It is a smile that is grounded in the peculiarly Oriental aversion to the more abstract flights and ethereal delights of Indian and Western peoples, and a preference for the concrete, this-worldly, ordinary-human, even 'trivial' moments of day-to-day existence. In fact, if one may speak of a special, and seldom appreciated, contribution of Asian peoples to world civilisation, it is to be found here: in this smile and what it symbolises.

A smile, of course, can mean many things. Here it may be said to represent a special sensitivity to the comic-mundane, a tender affection for even the commonplace things of life. Or – relative to the spiritual other-worldliness and mythological fantasy and philosophical grandeur of so many other cultures – it may be seen as a collapse of the sublime, an affirmation of unaffected naturalness and simplicity. As in the Tao of Lao-tzu, it is the smile of the child, and the smile of the sage.

It is in this soil, simple, earthy, pragmatic and humanistic in its most sophisticated forms, that the comic spirit of Zen is rooted, like the lotus flower that radiates from the lowliness of the mud at the bottom of the pond, and whose leaf-pads provide seats for all those little bullfrog Buddhas that are favoured in Zen art and poetry. In both its Chinese origins and its later Japanese elaborations, the development of Buddhism known as Ch'an and Zen owes much of its particularity to the distinctiveness of this Chinese and Japanese world-view. Out of the collision of the lofty spiritualism of Indian Buddhism and the earthiness of Oriental humanism and naturalism come both Zen and the comic spirit of Zen. For all of the austerities and rigours of Zen, and the serenity of its religious vision, in it the Chinese dragon smiles and the Indian Buddha roars with laughter.

> *Out from the hollow*
> *Of the Great Buddha's nose*
> *A swallow comes.*
>
> Issa[1]

The Zen tradition, in fact, according to legend, begins with a smile. This in itself, however apocryphal its basis, is a remarkable distinction in the history of religion, and profoundly suggestive of the character of Zen. Insofar as Zen has concerned itself with the question of its lineage, and of its relationship to the historical Buddha and his teachings, it has traced its ancestry not only to the awesome meditation master, Bodhidharma, or to the philosophically formidable figure of Nāgārjuna, but to one of the Buddha's disciples, Kāśyapa, whose principal distinction is that, at a critical moment, he smiled. According to the tale, when once the Buddha was gathered with his disciples, a Brahma-raja came to him with an offering of a beautiful golden flower, and requested that he preach a sermon. When the Buddha ascended his customary seat of instruction, however, he spoke no words to the expectant audience, but simply held up the sandalwood flower before the assembly. None of those present understood the Buddha's meaning, except for Kāśyapa who received the teaching instantly and acknowledged it with a smile.

This is the peculiar and profoundly symbolic origin attributed to Zen. And it is this smile, this sudden intuition of Truth, and this wordless transmission of the Dharma, that is said to have been handed down through twenty-eight Indian Patriarchs, the last of which was Bodhidharma who brought the doctrineless 'teaching' to China in the 6th century AD. The Buddha's silent gaze on Vulture Peak is the commencement of that propositionless communication of the innermost nature of things that is pivotal in Zen, that first and last word which cannot be spoken and which cannot be heard. This is the emphasis customarily and not incorrectly given to the Zen use of the legend. But the other aspect of the story is also important, and that is Kāśyapa's smile of understanding – a smile that is carried through in the subtlest to the most raucous forms throughout the later developments of Zen. This smile is the signature of the sudden realisation of the 'point,' and the joyful approval of its significance. It is the smile of Truth, or the Truth smiling. It is the glad reception of that moment of insight which has taken the whole world by surprise, a moment of seeing with the freshness and immediacy of the little child, full of amazement and wonder – a 'holy yea' which is capable of transforming even specks of dust into stars and frogs into Buddhas. And it is this smile, historically authentic or not, which is the beginning and end of Zen.

Bodhidharma and Pu-tai

Insofar as one can speak of fundamental images in a tradition that is so strongly non-symbolic and iconoclastic, there may be said to be two basic types of images in Zen, most noticeable at first in Zen paintings where they are constantly recurring, as if each calls forth and counterbalances the other. The one is the epitome of resolute seriousness; the other of buoyant laughter. The one is seated in the placid stillness of meditation; the other is airily dancing a folk-dance. The one suggests the extremities of earnestness and commitment; the other the carefreeness of gaiety, if not frivolity. The one presents the visage of the master or sage; the other of the child or clown or fool.

The first set of images in Zen is typified by the figure of Bodhidharma, determinedly facing the wall of a cave for nine years in intense meditation until, according to legend, his legs rotted off. Or Bodhidharma, accepting Hui-k'o as a disciple after the latter had cut off his arm in demonstration of his absolute sincerity and utter seriousness. Or Bodhidharma, confronting all would-be seekers of enlightenment like some fierce and formidable giant whose sheer presence overwhelms the staunchest defences of the ego. Or Bodhidharma, whose piercing eyes shoot forth like daggers from beneath shaggy brows set in a great craggy forehead, seeing through all the schemes of desire and the fortresses of ignorance.

The other set of images in Zen is typified by the figure of Pu-tai (Hotei, d. AD 916) who is even larger in bulk than Bodhidharma, yet more like an overgrown child, and no more awesome and fearsome than the pot-bellied 'laughing Buddha' which he becomes. Pu-tai, who refuses to enter a monastery on any basis suggestive of permanence, and instead wanders' freely without attachment even to the securities of cloistered walls and the forms of monkish discipline. Pu-tai who, like a carefree vagabond, carries a large linen sack from place to place as his only home. Pu-tai, whose jolly, roly-poly figure is to be seen dancing merrily, as if (as in Liang-k'ai's sketch, 13th century) floating gracefully in the air in spite of his size, seeming barely to touch the earth without leaving a trace. (See plate 3.) Pu-tai, whose religious life consists of playing with village children, as if life had now come full circle, as if the end were in some way a return to the beginning, as if even children and fools knew what priests and monks did not.

In consort with the herculean image of Bodhidharma is an impressive train of like figures, such as Lin-chi (Rinzai) with his lion's roar, snarling face and clenched fist, shouting and frightening monks directly into Nirvāna, as it were. Or Tē-shan (Tokusan) sitting almost menacingly, with his oak-stick poised in his lap, intently awaiting the precise moment when it will be needed for the collapsing of all categories (e.g., the Bodhidharma triptych by Soga Shōhaku, 15th century). Similarly, one may point to the two favourite Zen creatures, the tiger (or lion) and the dragon, which seem to have reincarnated themselves in so many Zen masters, and which, sharing in this same symbolism, serve as powerful animal emblems of the Zen sect.

Yet Pu-tai also has his retinue of attendant 'Bodhisattvas' and 'totems.' And a strange retinue it is. There are the two poet-recluses and monastery fools, Han-shan (Kanzan) and Shih-tē (Jittoku), with their boisterous, almost mad, and seemingly near-demonic laughter. And there are the three laughing sages of Hu-hsi, overcome with mirth in every painting, as if a Zen trinity were enjoying some eternal joke. (Plates 1 and 2.) Or there is Ryōkwan (1758–1831), the 'Great Fool,' as he called himself, of the Japanese Sōtō tradition who, like his Chinese predecessor and counter-part, delighted in playing games with children, or folk-dancing in the village. In fact, so absorbed would Ryōkwan become in this kind of 'zazen' that in one game of hide-and-seek he is reputed to have hid himself with such success under a haystack as not to be discovered until the next morning by a farmer!

Furthermore, this set of comic figures also has its favourite animals with which it, too, is associated, like the animal vehicles (*vāhanas*) of the Hindu gods. But instead of the tiger and dragon, in this case it is the monkey, or the frog, or the chicken, or even the louse! Liang-k'ai depicts Pu-tai in one painting as deeply and delightedly engrossed in a cock-fight, like a little boy hovering over a crucial game of marbles. Mu-ch'i, in addition to tigers and dragons, favoured monkeys, cranes and swallows. Sengai was fond of frogs. Indeed, one of his frog sketches carries the heterodox inscription: 'If by sitting in meditation (*zazen*) one becomes a Buddha . . . [then all frogs are Buddhas!].' (Plate 6.) Ryōkwan, among his many peculiarities, devoted special attention to lice, not only giving them a place of honour in his poetry, but sheltering them in his robe. And *haiku* verse – a literary oddity in itself – under Zen inspiration came to add a motley garden variety of lowly creatures to the sublime objects of aesthetic and religious representation: dogs, geese and carp; the thrush, the cuckoo, the sparrow and the crow; yes, and butterflies, fireflies, caterpillars, locusts, ants, bees and common flies.

> *Sitting like the Buddha,*
> *But bitten by mosquitoes*
> *In my Nirvāna.*
>   Demaru[2]

The tiger is now reduced to a house cat, grinning from the veranda. The dragon is gone, and in his place – a dragonfly.

> *He who appears*
> *Before you now – is the toad*
> *Of this thicket.*
>   Issa[3]

The set of images and symbols that cluster about the figure of Bodhidharma have been dealt with extensively in the literature on Zen. But what is one to do with this other set of images and symbols, especially when they, and their lowly animal 'vehicles,' are given such prominence in Zen legend, literature, poetry and art? What is their function and meaning in this curiously unfolding dialectic? What is it that they reveal? What mysteries do they open up? To what level of being and knowing do they point?

Most of what has been written about Zen, to phrase it as boldly as possible, is Bodhidharma Zen to the virtual exclusion of Pu-tai Zen; or dragon and tiger Zen apart from frog and flea Zen. Only occasionally in some writings, and never at all in others, does this dimension make its appearance and suggest its significance – as if it were only accidentally related to Zen, or perhaps not related at all. And in some cases, no doubt, this fairly accurately reflects the character of the Zen of a certain period, or school, or master, or interpreter; and especially when Zen is reduced to an orthodoxy or orthopraxy. Yet the images of Pu-tai, and his strange brethren, and his stranger menagerie of fellow-creatures, right down to the despicable louse, have persisted with the persistence of exhuberant children, chirping crickets and croaking frogs. And in their earthiness and unorthodoxy, their lowliness and commonplaceness, and in their playfulness and laughter and freedom, they continue to call attention to something very important, perhaps even supremely important, about both Zen and life.

In these terms, a basic Zen question – a *kōan* in its own right – is: What does Pu-tai symbolise? Toward what level of existence, into what kind of spirit, unto what insight and realisation, does he, and the odd train of figures that accompany him, like the Pied Pipers of an Oriental carnival, lead?

Half-a-person Zen

It is to be expected that some objection, perhaps even offence, will be taken because of the association suggested here, and frequently made hereafter, between Zen and the clown-figure and the comic-mundane, as if this were making light of, or ridiculing, or debasing Zen. Quite the contrary. This is not to detract or subtract from Zen in the slightest, but rather to add to it that dimension apart from which one is left with only 'half-a-person' Zen. Of course, if one understands Zen as simply a 'serious business' and therefore sees clown-figures like Pu-tai or Ryōkwan or Han-shan and Shih-tē, as threatening to a Zen so conceived, or if one understands the clown as being a peripheral, shadowy, base, or corrupting figure in relation to the priest or master or seer or sage, then this is correct. But there is far more depth and significance, yes, and spirituality in the clown than has commonly been recognised. He, too, belongs to a venerable tradition, and has an ancient history, and is no more intrinsically superficial or childish or base than the sacred personages which he often stands over against, parodies and counterbalances. If his function and meaning has suffered many abuses and misunderstandings, so has theirs. If his historical record and actual performance has often been coarse or dehumanising or even demonic, they are no exception either. But at his best and profoundest he, too, is a religious figure and a religious symbol. And in this role he stands at least on a par with all other religious *personae*, and, in some respects, even above them. For, as in the case of Pu-tai, he represents a larger spirit and a fuller, more embracing truth. The roundness of Pu-tai is the full circle of existence and the completed vision of life.

It is one of the peculiar distinctions of Zen in the history of religion to have appreciated this possibility, indeed necessity, and to have made it an integral part of the Zen experience and Zen perspective. Among the many unusual – though from the Zen standpoint perfectly normal – features of Zen is precisely that there is a singular and delightful at-homeness of the comic in Zen, and of Zen in the comic, an at-homeness which is surely remarkable and significant enough to be worthy of more extended treatment than it has heretofore been granted. And if this appears to be a way into Zen, and a way of Zen, which is strange and uncommon, it must be remembered that Zen masters themselves, as evidenced from the earliest anecdotal records, have often had some strange and uncommon ways of coming into Zen, and of pointing others to it: ways frequently eccentric and unorthodox, nonsensical and clownish, absurd and humorous. A tile falling off the roof and cracking the skull, the ping of a stone striking a stalk of bamboo, a slap in the face or a kick in the chest, a deafening roar or a rollicking guffaw, a single finger held up in silence or an enigmatic barrage of doubletalk: this is but a small sampling of the bizarre techniques and curious occasions for spiritual realisation that form the patchwork of Zen history.

What is being alluded to here, then, is not the clown as some inferior species, approaching the infantile or subhuman or chaotic, but the clown who in all his lowliness and simplicity and childlikeness, as well as in his iconoclasm and redemptive profanity, is truly great, truly profound, truly free. In this sense Pu-tai is a larger image of the Zen-man than Bodhidharma. For he is Bodhidharma having transcended the cave and returned to the light – and, as legend would have it, the very incarnation, in this lowliest of forms, of the Future Buddha, Maitreya.

Like all mysticisms, Zen is concerned to overcome certain dualities which are seen as splitting up existence, delimiting experience, and hiding true reality. But in overcoming such dualities, it is very easy to become caught up, perhaps quite unwittingly, in certain other dualities. These essays are concerned with just such 'other dualities', in particular those in which the dialectic of Bodhidharma and Pu-tai are involved: seriousness and laughter, sobriety and gaiety, holiness and humour, the dramatic and the comic, commitment and detachment, zealousness and frivolity, earnestness and disinterestedness, sense and nonsense, purpose and purposelessness, work and play. If the 'resolution' of Zen does not resolve this, then everything has only been resolved into yet another duality. And one is still left with only 'half-a-person' Zen.

Defeating the ego, desire, attachment and discrimination is one thing. Defeating the mentality of seriousness, labour and the dramatic alone is another – especially when the latter is seen as fundamental not only to the defeat, but also to the marking and maintenance of the victory over the former. If this is all that Zen achieves, then even the little child knows more than Bodhidharma. If this is the terminus of Zen, then even the fool is wiser than the supreme wisdom of the *Prajnāpāramitā*. For if Bodhidharma cannot laugh, it is because he has not seen through his meditation wall. If he cannot play, it is because he is still imprisoned in his cave. If he cannot dance, it is because his legs have indeed rotted off. (For a synthesis of Bodhidharma and Pu-tai see plate 4.)

The Master's Loud Roaring Laugh

Among the 1700 *kōans* which are said to be suitable for precipitating or deepening an inner spiritual illumination, and also for providing a test of its genuineness as an 'awakening', is the following question attributed to Hsiang-yen (Kyōgen, 819–914), and furnished with commentary by Wumēn (Mumon, 1184–1260) in his '*Gateless Gate*' to Zen Experience:

(Zen) is like a man up a tree who hangs on a branch by his teeth with his hands and feet in the air. A man at the foot of the tree asks him, 'What is the point of Bodhidharma's coming from the West [i.e., from India to China]?' If he does not answer he would seem to evade the question. If he answers he would fall to his death. In such a predicament what response should be given?

[Wu-mēn's commentary and verse]: It is as useless to be gifted with a flowing stream of eloquence as to discourse on the teaching in the great *Tripitaka*. Whoever answers this question correctly can give life to the dead and take life from the living. Whoever cannot must wait for the coming of Maitreya and ask him.

> *Hsiang-yen (Kyōgen) is really outrageous.*
> *The poison he brewed spreads everywhere.*
> *It closes the mouths of Zen monks,*
> *And makes their eyes goggle.*[4]

According to the later *Imperial Collection of Ch'an (Zen) Sayings* (1723–35), when Hsiang-yen first posed this *kōan* a leading monk, Chao, of another monastery who was present commented: 'I do not ask this question when the man is on the tree, but I ask it before he climbs up! Will the Venerable Master speak to this?' Whereupon Hsiang-yen gave a loud roar of laughter.[5]

In the elements of humour and laughter visible in such enigmatic *kōans* and *mondōs* (dialogues) and their witty commentaries and versified parodies is to be found but one of many examples of the important place granted to the whole spectrum of the comic in Zen. In Zen, too, in fact especially, there is a time to laugh and a time to dance, as well as a time to weep and to mourn (Eccl. 3:4). D. T. Suzuki has argued that 'Zen is the only religion or teaching that finds room for laughter.'[6] Though in relation to other religions this is, no doubt, an overstatement, in relation to Zen it is more of an understatement. For Zen does more than find room for laughter – which might, after all, mean only a very small and rarely occupied room at the back of the house. In a unique sense, the house of Zen *is* the house of laughter.

R. H. Blyth, with his penchant for dashing comment and characterisation, has defined the essence of Zen as humour.[7] Whether or not one might be satisfied to state the matter so bluntly, such an equation of Zen and humour nevertheless points to the possibility of interpreting Zen as that point in the movement of Buddhism from India to China and Japan in which humour comes to be most fully developed and self-consciously employed as an integral part of both a pedagogical method and an enlightened outlook – that is, both as one of the stratagems for realising enlightenment and as one of the consequences of enlightenment. Indeed, no more fitting token of this could be found than that of the 'loud roaring laughter' for which so many Zen masters have been noted, and which very early in the tradition becomes a favourite motif in both Zen literature and painting.

A standard phrase in Zen training, applied to a monk who is so ultra-serious about his disciplines and his 'Zennishness' that his very zeal and fanaticism is self-defeating, is that 'he stinks (or reeks) of Zen.' Over against what is seen here as bondage to earnestness, striving and sincerity, if not a bit of that old demon Pride, stands the commonly repeated phrase in the extensive corpus of Zen anecdotes, and the catharsis and wisdom which it brings: 'And the monk (or master) clapped his hands and gave a loud roar of laughter.' At the same time, as has already been intimated, three of the most frequently represented themes in Zen art are the gleefully dancing Pu-tai, the rotund embodiment of playfulness and mirth, the monastery fools, Han-shan and Shih-tē, bending over and laughing with hilarious abandon, and the 'Three Laughing Sages of Hu-hsi,' beside themselves in merriment.

This is particularly striking when one recalls that the Indian Buddhist scholastics, following the dramatic classifications of Bharata (4th century AD), carefully distinguished between six classes of laughter arranged in hierarchical fashion from the most sublime to the most sensuous and unrefined, only the most restrained forms of which were considered appropriate to the comportment of gentlemen and monks, and to the theatrical representation of such. The descending scale of categories in itself suggests that the fullest and most pronounced and enjoyable forms of laughter are *per se* at the furthest remove from both piety and propriety: *sita*, a faint, almost imperceptible smile manifest in the subtleties of facial expression and countenance alone; *hasita*, a smile involving a slight movement of the lips, and barely revealing the tips of the teeth; *vihasita*, a broad smile accompanied by a modicum of laughter; *upahasita*, accentuated laughter, louder in volume, associated with movements of the head, shoulders and arms; *apahasita*, loud laughter that brings tears; and *atihasita*, the most boisterous, uproarious laughter attended by movements of the entire body (e.g., doubling over in raucous guffawing, convulsions, hysterics, 'rolling in the aisles,' etc.).

Given this classification, obviously influenced by the ideals of aristocratic sophistication, it was understood that the first two types represented the restrained, polite laughter of the highly cultured and refined individual, the middle categories the moderate laughter of the average man, while the last two characterised the intemperate and vulgar laughter of the uncouth lower classes. The religious interpretation of this dramatic scheme followed suit, if it did not to some extent influence it. The first two forms approach the spiritual and the sublime; the last two descend into the crassness of the physical and the sensual, lowering and degrading the spirit. And, as might be expected from the logic of the system, and the presumed threat of laughter with respect to holy things, the Buddha was supposed to have indulged only in *sita*, the most serene, subtle and refined form of laughter.[8] It is almost as if to say that the Buddha was only 'guilty' of the first form of laughter!

To the puritanism of the pious imagination, and the humourlessness of the scholastic *lack* of imagination, it has always seemed unthinkable that the Buddha should have stooped to the 'barbarous' level of openly displaying the teeth in a

jovial grin, or of emitting even modest chuckles of amuse-
ment, let alone the more 'immodest' forms of hilarity. Yet
what is commonly found in Zen, so much so as not only to
characterise Zen but to be symbolic of it, is none other than
apahasita and *atihasita*, the loud, uproarious, unrestrained
laughter that is presumably at the furthest remove from the
delicate and scarcely detectable smile of the Buddha, and from
the placidity that Nirvāna represents. As Christmas Humphreys
has commented: 'There is more honest "belly laughter" in
a Zen monastery than surely in any other religious institution
on earth. To laugh is a sign of sanity; and the comic is deliberately used to break up concepts, to release tensions and to
teach what cannot be taught in words. Nonsense is used to
point to the beyond of rational sense.'[9]

While it may be true at a preliminary level that, as one
Japanese *senryu* puts it, 'the man who giggles is omitted from
the selection for the ambush,'[10] it is also true at another level
that the man who is incapable of laughter, and of seeing the
humour in his situation, is both trapped by his own ambush
and omitted from the celebration that follows the ambush.
Zen is a kind of ambush undertaken against the traditional
Buddhist 'devils' of ego, ignorance, desire, attachment and
bondage. But what a strange ambush it is! The peculiarity of
the Zen onslaught and surprise is that it is often undertaken
in the spirit and with the weapons of the comic rather than the
dramatic, in laughter as well as seriousness, and therefore
stands from beginning to end within the comic parenthesis.
As Yüan-wu (Engo, 1063–1135) commented with respect to a
Zen episode which culminated, like so many Zen episodes, in
the master's hearty laugh: 'His laughter is like a cool, refreshing breeze passing through the source of all things.'[11]

Thus, while one may be accustomed to seeking for signs of
enlightened attainment in the sober features of deep meditation and intense absorption, in Zen one may like as not be
presented with images of gaiety, lightheartedness and mirth.
Where we expect a representation of determined resolution and
grave demeanour, we are often given instead a picture that

seems to suggest profanity more than piety, and frivolity
rather than zealousness. When intimations of sublime serenity
and unperturbable tranquillity are anticipated, we may in fact
be confronted with the raucousness of a laughter that seems to
shake the very foundations of the world – which, indeed, is
exactly what it does! For Zen is not only the tradition of the
overwhelming ferociousness of Bodhidharma, who seems to
pounce like a great Bengal tiger out of every ink-sketch to
break the arms and legs of unsuspecting monks, or like a
celebrated Chinese dragon summarily to devour all traces of
ego, desire and attachment. It is also the tradition of the jolly
Pu-tai, spurning cloistered confinement, dancing with innocent abandon, and playing with children in the streets, or of
the clamorous laughter and mad buffoonery of the monastery
fools, Han-shan and Shih-tē. And here, too, one discovers that
ego, desire and attachment have a way of getting themselves
broken and devoured in the realisation of some great Cosmic
Joke, and in the greatness of a Cosmic Laughter, which reveals
itself in the strange holiness and wisdom of these Holy
Fools.

This is, as it were, something of the little comedy that Zen
presents in relation to the whole of the Buddhist drama. In fact,
the initial impression when confronted with the classical
literature and artistic representation of Zen is that one has
searched diligently for a spiritual master only to find a figure
more akin to a court jester of Mahāyāna, or has thought himself to have entered the peaceful repose of the Monastery of
Eternal Rest, only to be greeted by shouts and roars seemingly
having more affinity with insane or drunken laughter and the
blows of a tavern brawl. Bharata's aristocratic and spiritualistic
schema seems abruptly to have been stood on its head! Yet it is
precisely this entire range of laughter, and the many related
categories of clownishness, nonsense, absurdity, foolishness,
playfulness, joking and humour, that have come to be en-
dowed by Zen with important religious functions and significance, and woven into a remarkable way of perceiving and
experiencing life.

There are things that even the wise fail to do,
  While the fool hits the point.
Unexpectedly discovering the way to life in the midst of death,
  He bursts out in hearty laughter.

Sengai[12]

Notes

1. Henderson, page 147.
2. R. H. Blyth, *Haiku*, 4 volumes (Tokyo: Hokuseido, 1949–52), **IV**, 49.
3. Henderson, page 142.
4. *Wu-mēn-kuan* (*Mumonkan*, 1229 AD), trans. Sohaku Ogata, *Zen for the West* (London: Rider, 1959), pages 97–8.
5. Charles Luk, *Ch'an and Zen Teaching*, 3 volumes (London: Rider, 1960–2), **I**, 131.
6. Suzuki, *Sengai*, page 147.
7. Blyth, *Oriental Humour*, page 87.
8. Bharata, *Nātya Shāstra*, **VI**, vv. 61–2. Cf. Shwe Zan Aung, *The Compendium of Philosophy*, a translation of the *Abhidhammattha-Sangaha*, rev. and ed. by Mrs. Rhys Davids (London: Luzac, 1910), pages 22–5.
9. *The Middle Way*, **XLV** (August, 1970), page 91.
10. Blyth, *Oriental Humour*, page 331.
11. Suzuki, *Sengai*, page 10.
12. *Ibid.*, page 134.

'The Dragon's Song' on the verso page, and the opening inscriptions for chapters 2, 5, 6, 7 and 8, are from *The Transmission of the Lamp*, translated by Chang Chung-Yuan, *Original Teachings of Ch'an Buddhism*, (New York: Pantheon, 1969), pages 78, 169, 141, 143 and 95, 69, 104, 203 respectively.

TWO   *Zen Masters and Clown Figures*

Monk: 'During my travels since leaving Chang-an,
I have never struck anyone with my staff.'
Chao-chou: 'That proves that the staff you were
carrying was too short.'
TRANSMISSION OF THE LAMP

One of the first impressions that one receives in reading tales of
the often unorthodox lives and ways of many Zen masters is
the peculiar correspondence between these figures and that of
the clown. Regardless of the problem of authenticity, and the
separation of legend from fact, this image is too common and
consistent to be dismissed as simply a popular embellishment
alien to the character and approach of the Zen master. Whether
in part fictional (and therefore still of great symbolic importance) or not, the historical records convey the persistent form
of a personality and role to which the designation 'clown' is
not inappropriate.

This is not to associate the concerns and intentions of Zen
transmission with a vaudeville performance, but rather to
indicate a level of comic freedom in which the Zen master
lived, and the eccentricity of the techniques which he frequently employed, through his own 'clownishness' or some
humorous artifice, in order to evoke the spiritual awakening
and development of his disciples. Nor is this to suggest a
clown-figure in the sense of the playful buffoon, or of clowning simply for the sake of clowning – though this, too, may be
involved. Rather, the term is used primarily in the sense of the
clown who by his queer antics and strange attire, or by his
'crazy sayings' and his 'divine madness,' gives expression to
the special freedom he has attained, and who in that freedom

reveals some truth through the outlandishness of his performance, or in some bizarre way becomes the agent of salvation in
a particular situation.

Zen 'Buffoonery'

One of the immediate precursors of the Ch'an tradition, for
example, Fu Ta-shih (Fu Daishi, 497–569), a layman, is said to
have been invited by the emperor Liang Wu-ti to expound the
Diamond Sutra. As soon as he had ascended the seat for his
exposition, the emperor listening intently, Fu Ta-shih rapped
the table once with a stick and descended from his seat. He
thereupon asked the startled emperor, 'Does Your Majesty
understand?' 'I do not!' the incredulous emperor replied.
Fu Ta-shih said simply, 'The Bodhisattva has finished ex-
pounding the sutra.'[1] On a later visit it is said that he presented
himself at the palace before the emperor wearing a hat, a monk's
robe and a pair of shoes, it being accepted practice that a monk
wears no hat, a Taoist no shoes, and a layman no monk's
robe.[2]

A similar tale is associated with Kakua, reputedly the first
Japanese to study Zen in China, who upon returning was requested to address the emperor of Japan concerning all he had
learned of this strange sect. Kakua produced a flute from the
folds of his robe, blew one short note, and bowing politely,
walked out.[3] This appears to be the only record that has been
preserved of Kakua. In stark contrast to the voluminous
writings of so many prominent philosophers and theologians,
East and West, Kakua left to posterity but one thing: a single
note on the flute.

Aside from the problem of legendary embellishment (or, in
this case, abbreviation), the seemingly endless proliferation of
like tales in Zen accounts is too conspicuous to be set aside as
peripheral to the nature and method of Zen. It is apparent
from the host of such anecdotes that have been preserved, and
used in subsequent Zen pedagogy, that not only are the early
masters depicted as commonly employing various comic techniques in their dealings with monks, laymen, and even local

and imperial dignitaries, but as themselves living in the spirit and style of comic freedom. Notorious for their peculiarities and eccentricities, odd in their behaviour, and unorthodox in their methods, the Zen masters often suggest something of the trickster, prankster, jester, clown and fool all rolled into one.

The Japanese traveller Ennin, who visited China from 838 to 847, having met Ch'an monks on several occasions, reported that they were 'extremely unruly men at heart.'[4] Though this appears to be an unsympathetic observation on the part of one who was a member of the T'ien-t'ai (Tendai) sect, and who may have misunderstood and misconstrued what he saw, it points to a trait which is nevertheless there. It is a trait which, in some respects, is reminiscent of that delightful, playful and sagacious attribute which Lin Yutang called 'the old roguery of the Chinese character.'[5] In other respects one is reminded of the peculiarities of the early Franciscan monks who claimed an affinity with wandering troubadours and clowns, such as Friar Juniper who wore a ragged cowl and was called a block-head by the people, yet who was seen as having special powers in relation to the Devil, and whose strange antics were accepted as the sign of some special insight and grace. A similar move-ment is also found among the Holy Fools of the Greek and Russian Orthodox Church: through a divine madness, whether real or affected, they became 'fools for Christ's sake' assuming the role of the clown as an authentic religious role, and in this way manifesting spirituality through acts of foolish-ness rather than piety. Selfishness and pride were conquered through an identification with the fool; and through comic exaggerations the folly of the people was dramatised and exposed.[6]

This is not to imply that all Zen masters are clown-figures or holy fools, or that all who achieve awakening within the tradition of Zen do so in the context of comic techniques. Rather attention is being called to a comic spirit and style which achieves its fullest acceptance and development, among Buddhist sects, within Zen, and to a remarkable procession of individualists – one might even say 'characters' – who often appear to be as much at home in the comic as the sacred. In perusing their biographies, and their *kōans* and *mondōs*, one has the distinct impression of being witness to a Buddhist circus. There is Hsüeh-fēng (Seppō, 822–908) who, like the clown that plays at juggling, used to toy with three wooden balls, and who, when a monk would come to him to learn of Zen and the Zen way, would simply begin rolling the balls about.[7] There is Shih-t'ou (Sekitō, 700–790) who, when anyone would ask him to interpret some aspect of Buddhism, would like as not reply, 'Shut your mouth! No barking like a dog, please!'[8] There is T'ien-lung (Tenryū, d. 9th century) who when Chu-ti (Gutei, 9th century), earnestly seeking the true path of the Buddha, solicited his direction, without comment simply lifted up one of his fingers.[9] There is Yün-mēn (Ummon, 862/4–949) who would frequently respond, whatever the question, by yelling, '*Kan!*' (No!), and Lin-chi (Rinzai, d. 867) who would shout the meaningless exclamation, '*Kwatz!*' (Ho!).[10] Ma-tsu (Baso, 709–788), also noted for his lion's roar, once shouted so loudly at a disciple that he was deafened for three days – and also thereby enlightened.[11] There is Tao-lin (Dōrin, 8th century) who was called the 'bird-nest master' because he did his *zazen* seated in the crotch of a pine tree, looking from a distance like a large magpie nest himself.[12] Or there is Te-ch'ing (1554–1623), noted for helping to revive the Ch'an sect in the Ming dynasty, whose adopted name was Han-shan (Kanzan), 'Silly Mountain.' The same tradition carries over into Japanese Zen, with such figures as Ryōkwan of the Sōtō sect. Apparently considered by nearby villagers to be bordering on lunacy, if not over the border, his name means literally, 'Great Fool'. It was he who, upon being confronted by a burglar in the predicament of being unable to find anything to steal in Ryōkwan's simple forest retreat, gave the man his clothes, and afterwards composed the poem:

> *A burglar failing to carry off the moon,*
> *It shines in from the window!*[13]

This motley parade of individuals with their strange behaviour and 'holy foolishness' seems to file almost endlessly through the voluminous accounts of the Ch'an/Zen masters. Though the purpose is, in a sense, quite serious and the setting acutely authoritarian, nevertheless the panorama has a distinct comic quality intrinsic to it. Through riddles and enigmas, through nonsense and insults, through scowling and laughter, ejaculation and silence, as well as through slapping, kicking and striking, the point is made in, to say the least, a most eccentric manner. It is almost as if one were watching the capers of a troupe of clowns in a carnival, or an ancient Oriental version of the slap-stick characters in a Marx brothers' film. But, as in all profound comedy, one soon discovers that the object of laughter is really oneself in the larger predicament and folly of man.

The familiar self-portrait of Hakuin (1686–1769), the pivotal figure of Japanese Rinzai Zen, is illustrative of the intentional projection on the part of a Zen master of the image of the fool. Hakuin does not sketch himself in the idealised form of an enlightened one, or even in the realistic image of an austere *zenji*, but as a bald, fat, cross-eyed and hunch-backed old man. (See plate 9.) The poem Hakuin inscribed above the portrait is even more revealing:

> *In the realm of the thousand buddhas*
> *He is hated by the thousand buddhas;*
> > *Among the crowd of demons*
> > *He is detested by the crowd of demons.*
> *He crushes the silent–illumination heretics of today,*
> *And massacres the heterodox blind monks of this generation.*
> > *This filthy blind old shavepate*
> > *Adds more foulness [ugliness] still to foulness.*[14]

A similar portrait, possibly by a disciple and bearing the same poem, depicts Hakuin as looking almost sheepishly, with pursed lips, out of the corner of his eyes – through all of which, however, one can detect the sagacious twinkle of one who was not easily fooled by sanctimony and pretension.[15] And in another sketch Hakuin goes so far as to give his meditating form the unmistakable shape and smirk of the pot-bellied Pu-tai. (See frontispiece.)

The figure of the clown which stands out here in relation to the person of the master emerges just as clearly in the various tales of Zen monks at the point of death. The classic instance is that of Teng Yin-feng (8th century) who, when he was about to die, asked, 'I have seen monks die sitting and lying, but have any died standing?' 'Yes, some,' was the reply. 'How about upside down?' 'Never have we seen such a thing!' Where-upon Teng stood on his head and died. When it was time to carry him to the funeral pyre he remained upside-down, to the wonder of those who came to view the remains, and the consternation of those who would dispose of them. Finally his younger sister, a nun, came and grumbling at him said, 'When you were alive you took no notice of laws and customs, and even now that you are dead you are making a nuisance of yourself!' And with that she poked him with her finger, felling him with a thud; and the procession carried him away to the crematorium.[16] In this way Teng, assuming what, from the remarks of his sister, was the not unfamiliar role of the clown, expressed his achievement of spiritual freedom, his liberation from a desperate clinging to life and anxiety over self, and therefore his transcendence of the problem of death. What was said by Il Pistoia of the famous Italian court-fool, Matello, on his death-bed could well be said of Teng Yin-feng: 'With him, even Death made sport.'[17] There is here an element of both a Promethean laughter in the face of death, and a comic freedom within the larger freedom of enlighten-ment. The realisation of an authentic liberation, as in so much of the Zen tradition, is attested by humour; and the symbol of that liberation is the paradoxical figure of the clown.

The clown in most cultures, in fact, symbolises emancipa-tion and freedom, even though not necessarily in the most refined or most spiritual sense. Often his antics are simply a retrogressive leap into the irresponsible freedom of the child, or a socially tolerated rebellion against virtue and authority. And partly because of this there is an understandable religious suspicion of the clown, and an attempt to restrict and contain his liberties and profanations. The clown, nevertheless, in his capacity to stand apart from the crowd, its conventions and mores, is a useful symbol, and indeed a herald, of the uninhibited spontaneity and joyful laughter of a spiritual freedom that lies beyond good and evil, not in regression but in transcendence, not in rebelliousness but in emancipation. As Enid Welsford characterised the peculiar role of the clown-fool: 'Under the dissolvent influence of his personality the iron network of physical, social and moral law, which enmeshes us from the cradle to the grave, seems – for the moment – negligible as a web of gossamer. The Fool does not lead a revolt against the Law; he lures us into a region of the spirit where, as Lamb would put it, the writ does not run.'[18]

In this we are given a hint, at least, as to the basis on which a recent master, Harada Sogaku (1871–1961), lecturing on the text of the third Case of the *Wu-mēn-kuan* (*Mumonkan*), could direct: 'My admonition, then: Be a great fool! You know don't you, that there was a master who called himself just that [Ryōkwan]? Now, a petty fool is nothing but a worldling, but a Great Fool is a Buddha. Śākyamuni and Amitābha are themselves Great Fools, are they not?'[19]

The Wisdom of Children and Fools

The clown-figure is also a favourite motif appearing throughout the history of Zen painting. Two of the most popular subjects are the 'Ch'an fools' or 'crazy beggars' Han-shan and Shih-tē of the early T'ang dynasty (7th century). Usually depicted together, as in Yen-hui's diptych of the 12th century, both are represented as holy fools indulging in an hilarious mad-cap laughter – approximating, in fact, the sixth, lowest, most boisterous and presumably un-Buddha-like laughter on the scale of the Indian scholastics. According to Zen accounts Han-shan and Shih-tē had the appearance of tramps, the demeanour of madmen, and the comportment of pranksters. Han-shan is characterised as dressed in tattered clothing, with a nest of birch-bark for a hat, and shoes too large for his feet –

the epitome of the clown. Frequently visiting the Kuo-ch'ing monastery at T'ien-tai, the temporarily tolerated visitor might be fed with the remnants from the monks' table. And when eventually ushered out of the monastery he would laugh and clap his hands delightedly in a rather ungracious exit, to say the least, by Chinese standards. He is also sometimes represented carrying a blank scroll in his hands, that is, instead of a Buddhist sutra. His friend, Shih-tē, whose name means 'picked up' and who was apparently an orphan, without name and lineage, also frequented the monastery and was noted for activities equally bizarre. One day, for instance, given menial work to do in the Buddha hall, he was caught sitting with the Buddha image, chatting as if in conversation with an old friend, and sharing in his offering meal.[20]

Outlandish as these comic heroes might appear in either a religious or an artistic setting, as Munsterberg comments, 'their carefree behaviour and seemingly foolish laughter is characteristic of Zen.'[21] A commonly recognised trait of fools is that they are a disguised form of the sage. There is an element of divine inspiration in their apparent madness. A mysterious power is witnessed in the strangeness of their conduct, and some ineffable truth seems hidden in their nonsense. Hence, the familiar acceptance of the fool in many societies as being possessed of a spirit, a vehicle for the inbreaking of some supranatural order, attested by his transcendence of ordinary canons of reason and behaviour. A fascinating power is sensed in his presence, which may be a demonic power or a disabling madness, threatening and malevolent, but which may also be a holy spirit and the lunacy of a higher wisdom. Here the babbling nonsense of the fool and the muteness of the mime (like Chu-ti's one-finger Zen and Han-shan's blank sutra scroll) both 'speak' that which cannot be expressed, the truth which is unutterable, and hence are fitting symbols of the 'wordless Dharma' which transcends not only all words but all intellectual description and appropriation.

The prevalence of such clown-figures in Zen painting is not accidental, for their unrestrained laughter points to a level of freedom and spontaneity that lies beyond the tensions and dualities of an unenlightened perception of things. The comic spirit and perspective manifest in Han-shan and Shih-tē is no ordinary or vulgar hilarity. It represents the achievement of a larger wisdom and a liberation from bondage to ego, ignorance, desire and attachment. Their peculiarity is not an invitation to eccentricity for its own sake; nor is it a necessary sign of awakening, the imitation of which distinguishes one as an 'enlightened one.' The idiosyncracies that identify them may or may not be present. And even when they are present they function primarily as symbols of freedom in the highest sense, not just any sort of liberty and frivolity. They certainly do not provide symbolic justification for the confusion of spiritual freedom with libertinism – the signal for which this has often become outside its original home; for licence surely has nothing to do with the rigours and sensitivities of Zen. Random and antinomian behaviour, at best, is no more than a regression to childish irresponsibility and self-indulgence – which is hardly what Han-shan and Shih-tē represent. Theirs is the Wisdom of Fools that has perceived the true nature of folly.

Another favourite clown-figure in Zen painting is Pu-tai (Hotei), familiar to Westerners as the jolly, pot-bellied, Happy Chinaman or Laughing Buddha readily available in curio shops. As such he is the most popular of the seven gods of luck. Historically he is identified with a wandering priest named Keishi or Cho Tai-shi (d. 916), who carried a large linen sack (hence the name Pu-tai) with whatever possessions he had, and who was popularly believed to be an *incognito* appearance of Maitreya Buddha.[22] He is usually pictured in the company of children, merry with laughter, and carrying in his linen sack fruits and sweetmeats for the little ones. In two early paintings attributed to Liang-k'ai he is shown in the one bending over, innocently and delightedly watching a cock-fight; in the other he is dancing gleefully in playful abandon. As Munsterberg describes him, 'the broad face is dominated by the overlarge laughing mouth ... The upper part of the body is reduced to a big globe-like head grinning above an enormous belly.'[23] He is the dialectical counterpart of the same large-headed and heavy-set image of Bodhidharma, with his scowling face and piercing eyes, his beetle-brows and fierce, terrifying countenance.

This relationship between the images of Pu-tai and Bodhidharma, as in the case of Han-shan and Shih-tē, is not a frivolity in opposition to discipline and order, and therefore inimical to it, but a frivolity which emerges out of the harmony of spontaneity and discipline. It is certainly not the strained or forced frivolity of trying to 'have a good time', of pretending to be carefree and spontaneous, or of affecting the image of freedom and gay abandon. It is not laughter over against seriousness and thus in aggressive and hostile tension with it, but laughter in tune with seriousness, and seriousness in tune with laughter. What is being symbolised by the dialectic of the sacred and the comic – or fierceness and frivolity – in Zen is not a new duality, but a new unity, a dynamic rhythmic harmony, as in the first principle of Chinese painting, *ch'i-yün* (vital harmony, spirit resonance). If the comic spirit provides a contrapuntal effect, as it were, it is not an antagonistic movement, and therefore simply discordant, but as an integral part of the unity and wholeness of the composition of life, like the Tao which manifests itself in the interrelationship between *yin* and *yang*.

According to legend Pu-tai refused the designation of Zen master, as well as monastic restriction, and instead walked the streets with his sack over his shoulder, giving gifts to children, and playing with them in the streets. Sometimes, in fact, he is pictured sitting inside his sack (his only home) peering impishly out. In fair weather he wore wooden clogs (rain-wear) and in the rain he wore straw sandals. Like an Oriental Santa Claus, he was the merry sage with a twinkle in his eye who had rediscovered the wisdom and freedom and laughter of little children. Whenever he met a fellow Zen devotee, he is reputed to have extended his hand, saying in childish fashion, 'Give me a penny.' Or if anyone would suggest that he return to a temple or monastery, or more formally instruct others in the Zen path, he would again reply, with an air of innocence, 'Give me a penny.'[24] Pu-tai represents, therefore, the Zen goal of recovering on a higher plane the spontaneity and naturalness and playfulness – the 'little Zen' – of the child. If Han-shan and Shih-tē symbolise the Wisdom of Fools, Pu-tai symbolises the Wisdom of Children. He is not a little like the commonly ignored image of Jesus who pauses to play with the children, despite his disciples' dismay, or who sets a little child in the midst of his all-too-earnest followers with the declaration: 'Unless you turn and become like children you will never enter the Kingdom of Heaven' (Matt. 18:3).

It is also significant that Pu-tai, as this strange wandering mendicant, comes to be seen as an *incognito* form of the Future Buddha, Maitreya, of the age to come. The exalted Maitreya manifests himself in the earthly form of the lowly clown, simpleton and fool, 'linen-sack.' This convergence between the Zen roaring laughter of enlightenment, the mythology of the coming Messianic Buddha, and his legendary *avatar*, Pu-tai, is captured in a Buddhist chant before Maitreya:

> When the big belly thunders with loud roars of laughter,
> Thousands of white lotuses rain through all the worlds.
> With his bag of cloth vast is he as the Universe;
> He will succeed the Buddha, preaching in Dragon Flower Tree
> Park.[25]

Here, in this remarkable religious chant, Maitreya is given the same comic form in a cosmic setting as that humble figure which he incarnates.

Of similar import is another favourite theme in Zen art, 'The Three Laughing Monks at Hu-hsi (Kokei),' treated by painters such as Shih-k'o, Kano, Bunsei, Soga Shōhaku and Sengai. Though not clown-figures as such, their use in Zen art is similar to that made of Pu-tai, Han-shan and Shih-tē. The reference is to the pre-Zen story of Hui-yüan (Eon, 333–416) who had, for thirty years, successfully kept a vow never to cross the bridge which separated his monastic retreat at Hu-hsi from the world beyond. But on one occasion, as he went to bid goodbye to some fellow hermits who had been visiting him, he inadvertently crossed the bridge with them whereupon all three began laughing heartily. Su Tung-p'o's words, added to Shih-k'o's version of the scene capture the epiphany of laughter and, as it were, the Great Cosmic Joke which the jovial trio has suddenly realised: 'The three of them are laughing in chorus; even their clothes, hats, shoes all have an amused air. The acolyte behind them is beside himself with laughter.'[26] This is not an invitation to laugh at the picture, but with it, to be thrust into the comic dimension of all existence, including one's own.

The clown-motif is, of course, not limited to these commonly represented types, but is extended in Zen painting to a wide variety of subjects and situations: Mu-ch'i's 'The Priest Chien-tzu Laughing and Playing with a Shrimp,' Sengai's 'Travelling Monk with a Crazy Poem (*kyōku*),' or Hakuin's 'Self-portrait,' to name but a few. Similarly, the various other subjects that Hakuin sketched were given much the same touch: the Buddha, Kuan-yin, Bodhidharma, Lin-chi, Daito, and other Zen notables. In addition to their sternness or serenity or gentleness, all seem to participate in and to reveal the comedy of a common humanity, and at the same time to have entered the laughter of the gods that lies beyond. All suggest that the demons of desire and attachment, ego and ignorance, may be exorcised through laughter, and point to a kind of cosmic laughter that is to be entered on the other side of this exorcism.

This attention paid to the clown-figure in Zen literature and art is especially indicative of the significance of the comic spirit and perspective in Zen in the light of the Chinese (and Japanese) emphasis upon reserve, decorum, tranquillity and subdued expression, and general aversion to extreme displays of gesture and emotion. As Rowley comments with respect to the influence of the Chinese tradition upon canons of subtlety in artistic depiction: 'When physical action was required, either in running, playing or fighting, the Chinese resorted to various methods for avoiding the violence of naturalistic portrayal. In children at play, no matter how delightfully they gambol, they look like little men dancing or acting, instead of falling into the rough and tumble of a Western painting ... Even a drinking bout approximates a discussion among scholars. Only demons, immortals and demon-quellers are permitted to kick and scream and rush madly about.'[27] On this scale many Zen masters, painters and subjects, not being in the category of the immortals (except in Zen terms), become the strange bedfellows of demons and demon-quellers. Perhaps the poem which Hakuin inscribed above his self-portrait was not mere coincidence:

> In the realm of the thousand buddhas
> He is hated by the thousand buddhas;
>   Among the crowd of demons
>   He is detested by the crowd of demons.

The Zen Artist-Eccentric

George Rowley, in discussing the principles of Chinese painting, makes the oblique comment, which remains undeveloped, that in the Chinese ideal, 'the true painter has much of the fool in him. Ku K'ai-chih excelled in buffoonery and Huang Kung-wang called himself the "Great Taoist Fool." Painters were expected to be foolish, crazy, cranky or eccentric ...'[28] Whether this is an accurate generalisation concerning Chinese artists as a whole, certainly it is applicable to the more unorthodox artists classified in the i-p'in (spontaneous, intuitive, untrammelled) category, and to the many like-spirited Zen painters. The eccentricities of many Zen painters and Zen paintings had their roots, not only in the kindred spirit of the Zen masters themselves, but also in the precedent of such pre-Zen Chinese eccentrics as Ku K'ai-chih (4th century AD). In his day it was said of him, 'K'ai-chih is compounded half of real madness, half of conscious buffoonery. One cannot understand him without making allowance for both.'[29] Of greater importance is the precedent of the subsequent *i-p'in* artists whose unorthodoxies of manner and technique are frequently matched by unorthodoxies of spirit and life-style.

Of these Wang-hsia (8th century), nicknamed Wang-mo (Ink Wang), is credited with one of the earliest and most unconventional approaches to art. According to Chu Ching-hsüan he was a wanderer with a 'wildness of nature' who used wine to creative advantage. 'When he was drunk, he would splatter ink on (the surface), laughing and singing the while. He might kick it, or rub it on with his hands, wave (his brush) about or scrub with it . . . [Then] he would follow its configurations to make mountains, or rocks, or clouds, or water.'[30] According to another authority he would even dip his head in the container of ink, and paint with his hair as a brush.[31] Of the same period is a more obscure individual, identifiable only by his family name Ku, who would first lay out dozens of pieces of silk, and after becoming tipsy would run around them, sprinkling ink and then colours. Afterwards he would cover the spots with a large cloth, and with someone sitting on it, would pull it around the room, finally fashioning the blotches and smears into mountains and islands.[32]

Records of other early ink-splatterers include Chang Chih-ho, who also imbibed as a preparatory method of releasing inhibitions, and who began by waving a brush over the silk in time to music, with his eyes closed or his head turned away to effect complete randomness;[33] Kuo Chung-shu, who 'worked in a style which no master had formed;'[34] and Tsē-jēn of Yung-chia, who 'started out by culling the best points in all the various schools and studying them; then he had a dream in which he swallowed several hundred dragons, after which his achievements were divinely wonderful!'[35]

There is also Chang-tsao 'who was able to wield two brushes simultaneously, making with the one a living branch and with the other a decaying trunk.'[36] And there is Li Kuei-chēn, a wandering individualist, who wore only a single garment summer and winter, and whenever asked about his behaviour 'would suddenly open his mouth wide and suck his fist, without answering.'[37] Of a very different sort is Mi-fei (11th century) – landscape painter, connoisseur, critic, and author of the *Hua-shih* (History of Painting) – who earned the distinction of 'crazy (Mi)' for his eccentricities. He is said, for example, to have once dressed in official cap and gown and knelt in a gesture of worship as an expression of his esteem for an unusually beautiful rock.[38] Mi-fei, too, did not favour delicate brushwork or fine silk, but often used the roughest instruments, such as a dry stick of sugar cane, a lotus-stem, or an old rag. He is chiefly noted for his use of dots rather than strokes, achieving the desired effect through an accumulation of dots, applied with a wet brush.[39]

Common to all was the peculiar technique called *p'o-mo* (splashed or spattered ink, including also blowing, wiping and smearing). The mere representation of forms in an attempted conformity to the lines and colours of the object is downgraded, along with the traditional rules for painting which emphasised technical skill and delicacy of refinement in such representation. This is seen as getting the form and the finesse without necessarily capturing the spirit and entering into the spirit of the subject – indeed becoming one with that spirit. A paramount position is thus accorded the first principle of *ch'i-yün* (vital harmony, spirit resonance) and its intuitive realisation and articulation. When Pi-hung asked Chang-tsao who his teacher in the art of painting had been, he replied, 'In externals I have taken as my model the creative process of Nature; within, I have the springs of [my own] heart.'[40]

As can be seen in this brief summary, the ideals of intuitive grasp and spontaneous expression of the *i-p'in* artistic approach integrate well with the immediacy, simplicity and naturalness of the *p'o-mo* technique. And both, in turn, synchronise admirably with like emphases in Zen practice and experience. It is no accident that the two traditions, the artistic and the religious, came to find themselves so suited to each other. Though the *i-p'in/p'o-mo* painters hardly represent the dominant image of the Chinese artist, whose painting was much more in conformity with the classical Six Principles advanced by Hsieh-ho

(5th century), and whose life-style was more in accord with the ideal of the gentleman scholar (*wēn-jēn*), it is in relation to such unorthodox precursors and contemporaries as this that such early Zen painters as Shih-k'o, Liang-k'ai and Mu-ch'i are to be seen. Liang-k'ai (Ryōkai, 13th century) was reported to be 'a jocular fellow who called himself "the crazy Liang"'[41] and also 'the crazy vagabond.'[42] Mu-chi (Mokkei, 13th century), most widely renowned for his 'Persimmons,' was described – and not particularly with favour – in the *T'u-hui-pao-chien* as 'fond of painting dragons, tigers, apes, cranes, wild geese in rushes, landscapes, trees, rocks and human figures; and he did them all in a free and easy fashion, dotting with ink. He expressed his ideas quite simply without ornamental elaboration. His way of painting was coarse and ugly, not in accordance with the ancient rules, nor for refined enjoyment.'[43] Shih-k'o (Sekkaku) of the Five Dynasties Period (906–60) is characterised by a later writer, Liu Tao-ch'un (11th century) in a somewhat different, though no more flattering, manner: 'He liked to shock and insult people and composed satirical rhymes about them, not unlike those of the comedy actors, some of which are still repeated ... He mostly represented old and rustic fellows of strange appearance and grotesque shapes so as to shock the proud and pretentious. The people of Hsi-chou were much annoyed at him ...'[44] A similar impression is given in Li Chien's account in the *Hua-p'in* of Shih-k'o's painting of 'The Court of the Jade Emperor':

> Shih-k'o was a highly independent character, always mocking and making fun of his contemporaries. His manner of painting was bold and free and he had no consideration for rules and patterns. That is why his figures sometimes are so hideously strange and queer. He painted some of the officials (or divinities) of the Water Palace with crabs and fishes attached to their belts in order to shock the people who looked at them. I have just seen a picture by him, of an old man and woman tasting vinegar; they are holding their noses and squeezing their mouths to show its bitterness ...

In the painting of the Jade Emperor he did not dare to introduce so many playful things [gambolling devils, disrespectful servants, etc.], yet he could not refrain from representing crabs hanging (from the girdles) so as to make people of later times laugh.[45]

Even the presumably serious matter of presenting an official portrait to the master (or, in Hakuin's case, of presenting portraits to himself!), as a token of reverence, esteem and appreciation, is sometimes turned into a comic and clownish affair. When a disciple once presented a portrait to master Chao-chou (Jyōshū, 779–897), Chao-chou responded in *kōan*-like fashion: 'If it is really a true image of me, then you can kill me. If it is not, then it should be burned!'[46] The peculiarities of Zen teaching and its occasions seem unending! A different tale is told of P'an-shan (Banzan, 8th century), a disciple of Ma-tsu (Baso), who had requested that a portrait be made of him. Several likenesses were presented to him by his disciples, none of which satisfied him as having captured the spirit of his person and teaching. Then one of his disciples came forward with the assurance that he could do what the others could not; thereupon he turned a somersault and left the room. This was accepted by the master as being the best portrait.[47]

It is often acknowledged that a part of the artist's specific freedom and role as an artist is to stand apart from the conventional masks, the official façades, the socially determined costumes and *personae*, and thereby perchance to step into and to reveal a more authentic humanity and reality. Being an artist, of course, can also become a social role, with its own masks and costumes and façades, only reduplicating the inauthenticity in another form. Nevertheless the ideal is for the artist to leave a conventional humanity in order to disclose the man behind the man and the world behind the world. This, in itself, places the artist in a curious conspiracy with the clown and fool, a conspiracy in which he too may appear as something of a clown or fool. The clown's function is to profane the boundaries and distinctions, the categories and hierarchies, in which we imprison reality and in the same act imprison ourselves. The endowment of all limits and differentiations and forms with seriousness and sacrality is an act of setting things apart, surrounding them with taboos, walling them in their sacred enclosures, setting up 'no trespassing' signs – all of which must periodically if not finally be broken through lest they absolutise themselves in a rigidity of forms, and suffocate that which they attempt to preserve and enhance.

From the perspective of the clown, who refuses to take any limitations and demarcations with absolute seriousness, the moat that protects the king's castle and his kingship is also the moat that imprisons the king. Hence, the neat patterns of rationality and order and value which we use to organise experience are confused and garbled by the clown whose motley patches, incongruous garb, curious accessories, and bizarre behaviour place everything in suspension. Form is turned into chaos, sense into nonsense, inhibition into spontaneity, rigidity into randomness. The clown does not fit into, indeed refuses to fit into, the patterns and structures of the conventional world. He represents another order of being. The clown gets everything wrong: his dress, his appurtenances, his decorum, his logic, his speech, his movements; yet in this wrongness is a rightness of another sort. In his foolishness is another level of wisdom.

It must also be added that, if the clown-fool has a special facility for calling into question the category of the holy, he likewise has a way of not taking the unholy with absolute seriousness either. He goes beyond the knowledge of good and evil, sacred and profane – whether the 'beyond' that is before or after. As in the figure of the clown-fool in Christendom of the Middle Ages and the Renaissance, though he is often seen (particularly by ecclesiastical and political authorities) as party to a strange alliance with the Devil, the demons and the forces of chaos, the demonic realm was also a part of his parody. It is an erroneous belief that the modern clown in Western societies had his origin in the Devil of the medieval miracle plays. The Devil, too, was dressed in the garb of the clown or fool;

evil was placed in the same comic parenthesis as good. If the clown played with holy things, he also played with unholy things. If he dabbled in chaos, he did not do so unambiguously or demoniacally. He entered the no-man's land, as it were, between the competing forces of cosmos and chaos, angels and demons, and therefore stood outside both as if both were *māyā*, as if both were dramatic yet comic participants in a great stage-play. He, therefore, as Enid Welsford argued, was the *punctum indifferens* who existed in a realm all his own beyond both sides of the drama, now seeming to take one side, now another, but ultimately neither. Sometimes he was Vice, sometimes Virtue, yet finally not Vice and not Virtue.

> This ambiguous position is the inevitable result of the peculiar character of the Fool. The serious hero focuses events, forces issues, and causes catastrophes; but the Fool by his mere presence dissolves events, evades issues, and throws doubt on the finality of fact. The Stage-clown therefore is as naturally detached from the play as the Court-fool is detached from social life; and the fool's most fitting place in literature is as hero of the episodic narrative, or as the voice speaking from without and not from within the dramatic plot . . .
>
> The tragic writer takes this world seriously and interprets it; the comic writer creates a new world, a world where bad people are harmless, where stupid people are merry, where Fate is transformed into a Puck-like Chance strongly biased in favour of those who have a sense of humour and a proper appreciation of cakes and ale . . .
>
> The Fool is an emancipator.[48]

Notes

1. *Pi-yen-lu (Hekigan-roku)*, case 68. R. D. M. Shaw, translator and editor, *The Blue Cliff Records* (London: Michael Joseph, 1961), page 212.
2. Luk, **I**, 144.
3. Paul Reps and Nyogen Senzaki, *Zen Flesh, Zen Bones: A Collection of Zen and Pre-Zen Writings* (Garden City: Doubleday, 1959), pages 60–1.

4. E. O. Reischauer, translator and editor, *Ennin's Diary* (New York: Ronald, 1955), page 210. This comment is made with reference to twenty Ch'an monks which he met at a Ch'an monastery.

5. *My Country and My People* (New York: Reynal, 1935), page 52 ff.

6. G. P. Fedotov, *The Russian Religious Mind*, 2 volumes (Cambridge: Harvard University Press, 1966), II, 316–43.

7. Blyth, *Zen Classics*, II, 47.

8. D. T. Suzuki, *Essays in Zen Buddhism*, 3 series (London: Rider, 1949–53), III, 46.

9. *Wu-mēn-kuan*, case 3.

10. Isshū Miura and Ruth Fuller Sasaki, *Zen Dust: The History of the Kōan and Kōan Study in Rinzai (Lin-chi) Zen* (New York: Harcourt, Brace and World, 1966), pages 82–3.

11. Wu, page 101.

12. Blyth, *Zen Classics*, II, 11.

13. D. T. Suzuki, *Zen and Japanese Culture* (New York: Pantheon, 1959), page 365.

14. Miura and Sasaki, pages 124–5.

15. Suzuki, *Japanese Culture*, plate 40.

16. Blyth, *Oriental Humour*, pages 93–4.

17. Enid Welsford, *The Fool: His Social and Literary History* (London: Faber, 1935), page 319.

18. *Ibid.*, page 321.

19. Lucien Stryk and Takashi Ikemoto, *Zen: Poems, Prayers, Sermons, Anecdotes and Interviews* (Garden City: Doubleday, 1963), page 98.

20. Suzuki, III, 145.

21. Hugo Munsterberg, *Zen and Oriental Art* (Rutland: Tuttle, 1965), page 34.

22. Henri L. Jolly, *Legend and Japanese Art* (Rutland: Tuttle, 1967), pages 120–2.

23. Munsterberg, page 55.

24. Reps and Senzaki, page 16.

25. Luk, I, 111.

26. Arthur Waley, *An Introduction to the Study of Chinese Painting* (New York: Scribners, 1923), pages 228–9.

27. George Rowley, *Principles of Chinese Painting*, 2nd edition (Princeton: Princeton University Press, 1959), page 17.

28. *Ibid.*, page 14.

29. Waley, page 48.

30. *T'ang-ch'ao-ming-hua-lu*, translated by Alexander C. Soper, *Archives of the Chinese Art Society of America*, IV (1950), page 20.

31. Cited in Chang Yen-yüan's *Li-tai-ming-hua-chi* (AD 847). W. R. B. Acker, *Some T'ang and Pre-T'ang Texts on Chinese Painting* (Leiden: E. J. Brill, 1954).

32. S. Shimada, 'Concerning the I-P'in Style of Painting, Part I,' translated by J. Cahill, *Oriental Art*, **VII** (Summer, 1961), page 69.

33. *Ibid.*, pages 68–9.

34. Alexander C. Soper, translator, *Kuo Jo-Hsu's Experiences in Painting* (Washington: American Council of Learned Societies, 1951), page 44.

35. *Ibid.*, page 61.

36. *Ibid.*, page 81.

37. *Ibid.*, pages 28–9.

38. Lin Yutang, *The Chinese Theory of Art* (New York: Putnam, 1967), page 98.

39. Yee, page 158.

40. Soper, *Kuo Jo-Hsu*, page 8.

41. Osvald Sirén, *Chinese Painting, Leading Masters and Principles*, 7 volumes (New York: Ronald, 1956–8), **II**, 11.

42. Munsterberg, page 53.

43. Sirén, **II**, 138.

44. Sirén, **I**, 161.

45. *Ibid.*, pages 163–4.

46. Wu, page 144.

47. D. T. Suzuki, *The Zen Doctrine of No-Mind* (London: Rider, 1949), page 86.

48. Welsford, pages 324–6.

THREE   *The Buddha and the Bullfrog*

An old pond.
A frog jumps in.
Plop!
BASHŌ

Santayana argued that at the heart of comedy lies a confusion of categories ordinarily kept distinct, like applying the formulae of theology to cookery or of cookery to theology.[1] Comedy is therefore a trespasser upon the holy ground of spheres which we expend a great deal of energy in defining and keeping separate, only to have them thrown back precipitously into the same knapsack with odd bits of everything. The king is forcibly tossed by the court jester into the street with the beggar. The Bodhisattva is suddenly indistinguishable from the novice monk. Gods and goddesses are made to consort with common animals. And the Buddha is placed in the lotus pond along with the frogs.

This is the comedy of the scroll-scenes (*chōjū-giga*, or animal caricatures) traditionally assigned to Toba-sōjō (1053–1140) in which monkeys, foxes, rabbits and frogs take the place of monks, priests and laymen in Buddhist ceremonies, as well as in a variety of secular activities. In one of the delightful culminating scenes of the first scroll, a monkey officiates as head priest in a temple service, praying before the altar of a large bullfrog Buddha seated on a 'lotus' throne made of cabbage leaves.[2] (See plate 5.) Though these are not Zen sketches – Toba-sōjō having been a priest and 'bishop' of the T'ien-t'ai (Tendai) sect – they are of the same order as many Zen works and serve to indicate that Zen was not alone in its appreciation for the importance of the dialectic of the sacred and the comic, religiously and aesthetically.[3] In Zen, however, the employment of this dialectic is more consistent throughout its history, more central to the tradition, and often more radical. In correspondence with the thorough-going iconoclastic temper of Zen is an equally thorough-going emphasis upon the mundane, the ordinary and everyday, the human, which constantly manifests itself in Zen literature, art and life.

The Collapse of the Sublime

Dating from the 9th and 10th centuries, Zen painting, like Zen literature, instruction, meditational practice and monastic life, marks a distinct break from the typical, Indian inspired, Mahāyānist Buddhist themes, scenes and subjects. As Osvald Sirén comments, Zen painting generally 'had very slight, if any, connection with traditional forms of Buddhist art.'[4] In place of the glorified and exalted Buddhas and Bodhisattvas, elegantly and royally attired, awesomely displaying their superhuman powers and surrounded by a host of heavenly beings and lesser spirits, are the extremely plain, earthy, unmistakably human sketches of the Buddha, Bodhisattvas, Arhats, and various Zen masters and patriarchs. The figures are often very powerfully represented, as in the numerous portrayals of the founder, Bodhidharma. But it is a very thisworldly power, immediately open to the self-realisation of all men, and the total effect is that of very simple and mundane figures. The 'portraits' of Bodhidharma, or even Śākyamuni himself, are the antithesis of the magnificent imagery familiar from early Chinese caves such as Tun-huang and Yun-kang,[5] or early Japanese temples like Hōryūji[6]: Amitābha (Amida), the Saviour-Buddha, beckoning from the paradisal splendour of his Pure Land; Kuan-yin (Kwannon), goddess of mercy, and the seemingly endless multitude of other benevolent Bodhisattvas, offering their treasuries of grace and merit; or Maitreya (Miroku), the Future Buddha, holding forth the promise of his coming dispensation. As Suzuki put it with respect to the transformation of Mahāyānist figures in Zen:

'Both Kwannon and Monju [Mañjuśrí, Bodhisattva of Wisdom] were brought down to the market or the woods or anywhere we humans were accessible. Kwannon was pictured with a basket filled with fish; Monju came out to our world accompanied by the monkey or the crane.'[7]

R. G. Collingwood argued in his aesthetics that 'the theory of laughter belongs to the philosophy of art; the satisfaction which we find in it is an aesthetic satisfaction, and to this extent the comic is a form of the beautiful ... A mere collapse or disappointment is not comic; it must be an aesthetic collapse, a collapse of the sublime.'[8] Zen art hardly signals a disappointment, but it definitely signals a collapse of the sublime, and does so both aesthetically and religiously. This is the reason – or one of the reasons – why the comic spirit and perspective is so much at home in Zen and Zen art; for one of the functions of comedy is to bring everything back to earth, if need be by making things fall into the mud. And the very juxtaposition of the gorgeous, heavenly Buddha, arrayed in his radiant power and glory, with his lavishly decorated and richly costumed Buddha-field, or the awesome thousand-armed and thousand-eyed Avalokiteśvara, or the overwhelming multitude of compassionate Bodhisattvas, with the perfectly plain and unpretentiously humble figure of Bodhidharma facing the wall of his cave (Sesshu), or of the Fifth Ch'an Patriarch carrying his hoe (Mu-ch'i), or the Sixth Patriarch bending over, cutting a stalk of bamboo (Liang-k'ai), is itself comic, quite apart from any specific inclusion of comic motifs or effects.

This is just as true whether one takes the type of portrait that becomes official from the 13th century on, in which Bodhidharma is pictured as burly, stern and awesome, with heavy brows and piercing eyes, and a visage suggestive of a tiger or dragon, or the slight, rather ordinary, and more compassionate-appearing patriarch found in the manuscript illustrations of the *Chuan-fa-chēng-tsung* (*ca.* 1054) and the palace roll of figures painted by Chang Shēng-wēn (*ca.* 1176) – although the former treatment tends more toward caricature and lends itself more to comic subtleties.[9] In either case, as Suzuki put it, Zen 'took away from Buddhist figures that aloof, unconcerned, rather unapproachable air which had hitherto characterised them. They came down from the transcendental pedestal to mingle with us common beings and with common animals and plants, rocks and mountains.'[10] The divine became human, as it were, in its peculiarly mundane and profane Zen form as the dimension of Buddha-nature (*Buddhātā*) in all human beings, indeed in all things.

The radicalism of the Zen transformation is even more striking when compared with the magnificent imagery of the Mahāyānist sutras, which provide the literary counterparts of such artistic splendour and profusion. In one of the Pure Land sutras, for example, the wondrous form of Amitābha is offered to the devotee as an object of contemplation:

> His body is coloured like the pure gold in a hundred, a thousand, ten thousand and a hundred thousand Yamalokas [Yama heavens], (with the height of) as many yojanas as there are sand grains in six hundred thousand lacs of nayutas [millions] of Ganges rivers. The white hair between his eyebrows curls five times to the right like five Mount Sumerus. His eyes are like the water of four oceans with the blue and white clearly distinguishable. The pores of his body send out rays of light as great as a mount Sumeru. The halo (round his head) contains a hundred lacs of great chiliocosms [billion worlds] wherein appear Nirmānakāya Buddhas as many as there are sandgrains in a million lacs of nayutas of Ganges rivers. Each Nirmānakāya Buddha has a following of countless Transformation Bodhisattvas serving him. Amitāyus Buddha has 84,000 marks; each mark has 84,000 excellent characteristics; each characteristic sends out 84,000 rays of light; and each ray of light illumines and attracts to it all living beings in all the worlds in the ten directions who (earnestly) think of him.[11]

In relation to this fabulous immensity and overwhelming brilliance the Zen treatments of the Buddhas and Bodhisattvas, insofar as they are treated at all, appear as if starkly and nakedly human, abruptly and unceremoniously stripped as it were of all mythical fantasy, regal splendour, and preternatural glory. As Suzuki says of the equally marvellous Buddha of the *Gandavyūka*: 'He no more sits on a high seat decorated with seven kinds of jewels, discoursing on such abstract subjects as Non-ego, Emptiness, or Mind-only. On the contrary, he takes up a spade in his hands, tills the ground, sows seeds, and garners the harvest. In outward appearances he cannot be distinguished from a commoner whom we meet on the farm, in the street, or in the office ... The Buddha in his Chinese Zen life does not carry his *Gandavyūka* atmosphere ostentatiously about him but quietly within him.'[12]

The same inversion occurs with respect to other orthodox Buddhist themes and scenes. In place of the depiction of the seemingly inexhaustible *Jātaka* episodes from the life of the Buddha and his previous incarnations, or the profusion of myths associated with the host of other Buddhas and Bodhisattvas, or the variety of levels and tortures in Buddhist hells and the correspondingly extravagant Paradise scenarios, Zen painting, like Zen literature, offers the this-worldly landscapes and commonplace events of everyday life: Ma-yüan's 'Old Man Asleep in a Boat,' 'Man Fishing,' or his 'Monks Playing Chess in a Bamboo Grove' (12–13th century); Liang-k'ai's 'Sixth Patriarch Cutting Bamboo,' or his 'Monk Eating Pig's Head' and 'Monk Playing with a Shrimp' (13th century); Mu-ch'i's 'Monkeys,' 'Swallows' and 'Persimmons,' or his 'Priest Sewing his Mantle' (13th century); Yü-chien's 'Mountain Village in Clearing Mist' (13th century); Mo-kuan's 'Four Sleepers' and 'Kingfisher' (14th century); or Josetsu's 'Fishing for a Catfish with a Gourd' (15th century). This not only reflects a movement away from stock religious themes and pious devotional images – Buddhas, Bodhisattvas, gods and goddesses, monsters and devas, mythological episodes – but the admission of almost any aspect of existence as a legitimate religious theme and artistic subject. The sacred cosmos is profaned in order that the sacredness of the 'profane' world might be revealed.

This is not to suggest that the conventional Mahāyānist motifs are never treated by Zen artists. But they are certainly no longer dominant motifs, and even when they are treated it is in a distinctively this-worldly, concrete and ordinary-human manner. As in Ch'ēn-hsien's (17th century) illustrations of Śākyamuni, Kuan-yin, Arhats, monks and priests, the treatment does not, as Sirén puts it, 'always seem to be as reverential as the traditional motifs might imply . . . [He] has transformed the saintly men into ordinary human beings divested of their holiness.'[13] In Suzuki's words, 'The Chinese practical genius has brought the Buddha down again on earth so that he can work among us with his back bare and his forehead streaked with sweat and covered with mud. Compared with the exalted figure at Jetavana surrounded and adored by the Bodhisattvas from the ten quarters of the world, what a caricature this old donkey-leading woman-Buddha of Shoushan, or that robust sinewy bare-footed runner of Chih-mēn!'[14]

The same may be said of the Mahāyānist paradises, as exemplified in the magnificent murals of Hōryūju, which presented the four paradises of the four directions, with Śākyamuni's paradise in the south, Amitābha's in the west, Bhaisajyaguru's in the east, and Maitreya's in the north.[15] Paradise, for Zen, is immediately accessible and is indistinguishable from the world of ordinary perception – though not as ordinarily perceived. It is not to be located in some other world, nor in a world which one enters by closing the eyes and shutting out the mundane and the commonplace, nor a world which by its holiness and infinity and brilliance devalues this world, empties it, and renders it impure, drab and profane. It is not the world at the end of the rainbow of fantasy and mind-expansion, or at the furthest remove from this world. As in the T'ang master Yēn-yang's (Gonyō) characterisation of such Buddhist fundamentals as the Three Jewels (Buddha, Dharma and Sangha) and the corresponding Three Refuges ('I take refuge in the Buddha; I take refuge in the Dharma; I take refuge in the Sangha'), it is the world in which 'the Buddha is a mass of clay, the Dharma is the moving earth, and the Sangha is one who eats gruel and rice.'[16] Or as Eicho commented, referring to the contemplative image of the Buddha as golden in colour and sixteen feet in height: 'Zen makes a humble blade of grass act as the Buddha-body sixteen feet high, and, conversely, the Buddha-body sixteen feet high act as a humble blade of grass.'[17]

If one moves from subject matter to style, the same mundaneness and unpretentiousness is evident. The Zen style, so clearly reflected in the techniques and effects which it utilises, is not the extravagant, the luxurious, the ornamented, not the riotous display of lines and colours, nor the seemingly endless proliferation of subjects and objects filling every particle of space, but the plain, unadorned, suggestively sketchy strokes of the brush, the aversion to detail – let alone adornment – and the impressionistic capture of moments of fleeting experience. In relation to the extravaganzas of Mahāyānist art which had made its way into China from India, Zen art represents a determined refusal to indulge in the embellishments and profusions of mythological fantasy or the ornateness and splendour of the pious imagination, hardly in fact even to indulge in colouration at all, with its decision to return, most frequently, to the earlier, non-Buddhist, Chinese monochromatic tradition of painting, stemming from calligraphy, and its favouring of the unorthodox *i-p'in* style and *p'o-mo* techniques.[18]

Whether, therefore, in terms of subject matter or style, it is the kind of art world in which, as it were, court jesters are much more at home than their kings and queens, buffoons than their lords and ladies, and in which priests and devotees look more out of place than clowns and fools, or for that matter than birds, fish and frogs. It is the kind of world in which Hakuin can sketch a scene of a Zen priest urinating, or Sengai engage in the grossness of his 'One Hundred Days Teaching of the Dharma.' (See p. 106.) It is the kind of world in which it is not inappropriate for both Hakuin and Sengai to accompany their works 'crazy verses,' or for Sengai to substitute himself for the Buddha in the most sacred *Parinirvāna* scene. And lest this should appear to be an example of a low point in Buddhist spirituality, it must be remembered that Hakuin was one of the most significant and prominent masters in the history of Japanese Zen, and that Sengai, a great master in his own right, was only giving expression in ink and verse to an unusually profound appreciation for the significance and sacrality of even the lowliest and most 'profane' aspects of life. When confronted with such individuals it is easy to react, as does Munsterberg, with the customary misgivings of aestheticians and religionists when faced with similar phenomena: 'It is on this note that Zen painting drew to its close – a note of gaiety and charm, no doubt reflecting the decline which Zen had suffered in modern Japan.'[19] One might just as well have said, 'reflecting the decline which brought Zen into being,' i.e., the collapse of the sublime.

Overcoming Sacred and Profane

So thorough-going is this collapse of the sublime that it has been seen by some interpreters as the result of secularising tendencies, either in Chinese culture in general or Zen in particular. It is to be acknowledged that there are certain historical realities which have some part to play in this shift. The various persecutions of Buddhists, the most devastating of which was that of Emperor Wu-tsung in the years 842–45, were misfortunes which a radical Zen iconoclasm, and a Zen incorporation of much of the Chinese outlook and sensibility, were exceptionally well-suited to weathering. And Zen itself was not unrelated to the corresponding resurgence of an emphasis upon indigenous Chinese thought and culture, with its distinctively this-worldly and humanistic character, over against alien forms of Indian spirituality.

In dealing with Zen one must pay special tribute to the very practical, realistic and moderate character of the traditional Chinese philosophy of life which would not accept Buddhism apart from a stress upon the mundane and the human. Highflown metaphysics and extended forays into other-worldly spheres of pious speculation and yearning must often have appeared as 'much ado about nothing' before the realism and common sense of the Chinese perspective, informed as it was by both Confucianism and Taoism. In Hu Shih's well-known description of the context out of which Zen emerged: 'The Chinese mentality is practical and abhors metaphysical speculation. All the religions and philosophies of ancient China were free from the fantastic imaginativeness and hair-splitting analysis and gigantic architectonic structure which characterise all religious and philosophical literature in India. When China was brought face to face with India, China was overwhelmed, dazzled and dumbfounded by the vast output of the religious zeal and genius of the Indian nation. China acknowledged its defeat and was completely conquered. But after a few centuries of bewilderment and enthusiasm, the Chinese mentality gradually reasserted itself and began to search for those things which it could really understand and accept. It now undertook to sift from this vast literature of Buddhism those elements which might be regarded as essentials in distinction from the impressive images and grandiose rituals and unintelligible metaphysics and superstitious charms and spells.'[20]

The kind of secularity and humanism and good-humoured matter-of-factness that has always graced Chinese culture, and that is early manifest in such a delightful manner in Chuang-tzu, is now manifest in the happy marriage of Taoism with its Chinese dowry and Buddhism with its Indian legacy, the offspring of which is Zen. 'There is no question that the kind of thought and culture represented by Chuang-tzu was what transformed highly speculative Indian Buddhism into the humorous, iconoclastic, and totally practical kind of Buddhism that was to flourish in China and Japan in the various schools of Zen.'[21] This Chinese contribution to Zen of the mundane and the comic is illustrated, perhaps as well as by anything, in Lin Yutang's comment that 'Chinese scholars always bequeath to us so many collections of "notebooks" ... consisting of unclassified paragraphs, in which opinions on the authorship of literary works and corrections of errors in historical records are mixed up with accounts of Siamese twins, fox spirits and sketches of a red-bearded hero or a centipede-

eating recluse.'[22] This is very much, in fact, an apt description
of what a collection of Zen paintings or of Zen anecdotes looks
like.

Chinese art and literature, generally, reflects a devoted
attention to the endless variety of this-worldly objects, a con-
geniality to even the lowliest creatures and most common
particulars of day-to-day existence. The whole range of earthly
life is opened up as if, in itself, a sacred mystery, as if in its very
miscellaneousness the proper locus of reverent attention, and
as if the true paradise, realistically perceived, were to be found
in the beauty and refined awareness of the 'pure land' immediately available to experience. The most cursory glance at a
collection of Chinese, as well as specifically Zen, paintings, or
a skimming of the classical records and accounts, reveals the
same detailed surveillance of the menagerie of ordinary delights. There is Chang Sēng-yu who is remembered for his
snow scenes; Chou-fang for his court ladies; Pien-luan for his
birds and flowers. Han-kan excelled in horses, Chang-hsüan in
women and girls, Han-huang in oxen, Tai-sung and Tai-i in
buffaloes. Fēng Shao-chēng is noted for his dragons and birds,
Sun-wei for his dragons and turbulent water. Li Ai-chih's
specialty was cats. Hsu-hsi's forte lay in flowers, butterflies
and garden vegetables, including cabbages; Mei Hsing-ssu's
was barnyard fowl. Prince Chün was eulogised for his treatment of bamboo, and also as a 'clever painter of shrimps,'
while the prince of Chiang-tu was acknowledged as an
'expert painter of sparrows, cicadas, and donkeys.' Ch'i-tan
was at his best in 'the hairpins and hatstrings of the Court,' and
Fa-shih in 'picknicking noblemen.' K'uai-lien was especially
fond of cranes, and Ts'ui-k'o remarkably captured the subtle
distinctions between hares.[23]

The recognition that Zen adopts rather than creates this
climate does not, however, in the least depreciate the contribution of Zen itself; for the primary context of Zen was still
religious and Buddhist. And, in relation to the established conventions and treatments of this tradition, Zen self-consciously
turned away to more 'secular,' mundane and comic forms of

art and literature. To be sure there is here a kind of secularisation process at work in Zen, which on one side is a purging of holy things and lofty compositions of their special sanctity and sublimity. Yet at the same time this process takes place in a religious context, and involves a sanctification of its own: the sacrilising of the earthy, the human, the commonplace event, the 'meanest creature and flower.' As in the practice, dating from the earliest Zen monasticism, the master meditates and teaches and guides; but he also participates, like everyone else, in building, cultivation, cooking, sweeping and washing. The one activity is not sacred, and the other secular; rather, the distinction has been transcended. Indeed, particularly from the viewpoint of the Southern, Sudden Enlightenment School, it is just as possible to achieve enlightenment in the act of cleaning as in meditating or studying the sutras.

There is, of course, the story of the prominent 11th-century painter, Li Lung-mien, who was warned by a (Ch'an?) monk[24] that if he continued to paint so many horses he would be reborn as a horse, whereafter, it is said, he began to deal with more obviously religious themes! As the evidence suggests that he nevertheless continued to paint horses, and other 'secular' matters, in his later years, the anecdote either originated in a jest or was the apocryphal invention of a Buddhist attempt to situate his religious works in his mature years.[25] Even in dealing with religious themes, however, Li was apparently instrumental in mellowing and further humanising the earlier manner of representing Arhats (which was in itself quite thisworldly), softening the severity and grimness of their features, replacing the 'rather terrifying old men with their ravaged and foreign [Indian] features ... by more pleasant-looking, wellnourished monks of a rather jovial appearance.'[26]

The effect of the Zen achievement is not secularisation as such, but a kind of spiritual democratisation of things in which the categories of importance versus unimportance, value and valuelessness, profundity and triviality, wisdom and simplicity, beauty and ugliness, good and evil, sacred and profane, no longer apply. Or, to put it more positively, it is a revaluation of things in which the distance between great and small, lofty and lowly, powerful and weak, magnificent and plain, extraordinary and common is reduced to nothing, permitting a magnanimousness of spirit in which even the humblest and poorest and dullest of creatures is seen as having its own significance and value. The exalted is humbled, and the humble is exalted, as it were. A dualistic way of thinking which arranges things and compares things and separates things, and which interposes its classifications between the experiencer and the experienced, is toppled. As master Kuei-shan (Isan, 771–853) remarked: 'When all feelings about the saintly and the profane have been wiped out, there will be exposed the body of true eternity.'[27] In the same way Hui-nēng (Enō, 637–715) instructed his disciples: 'If someone asks you about the meaning of existence, answer him in terms of non-existence. If he asks about the worldly, speak of the saintly. If he asks of the saintly, speak of the worldly.'[28]

Such a perspective can, of course, be viewed as a very serious and sobering one. Yet, like the collapse of the sublime, it is also at the heart of the comic perspective. The clown and the comedian have often functioned at their best as the great levellers in relation to all hierarchies and all distinctions, however sacred. Through overturning, or puncturing or collapsing, or standing things upside down, they effect a reversal or 'flattening' of categories and discriminations, the result of which is closely akin to that sense of unity and fellow-feeling, that oneness or identity of all things that mystical experience realises. And it is in this sense, too, that Zen masters and artists have commonly performed the clown's role in relation to and within the larger Mahāyāna tradition. If the dualities and oppositions such as beauty and ugliness, sacred and profane, truth and error, are seen as a part of the spiritual problem, it has always been a primary function of the clown and the fool to annul just such distinctions by reducing the sublime to the ridiculous, by profaning the sacred, by turning reason into nonsense, by giving the prize to the ugliest man in town. Theirs is the Emersonian motto: 'I unsettle all things.

No facts are to me sacred, none are profane.' The precious gem is treated as a common pebble, while the common pebble is fondled as a precious gem.

The mystical goal of bringing about a collapse of categories, curious as it may seem at first sight, is also the intent of the comic spirit. In some respects it intensifies the categories and contrasts as a mock prelude to collapsing them. The beauty is placed with the beast, the king is made to walk hand in hand with the beggar, the wise man and the village fool are put side by side in the seats of honour, and the Buddha and the bullfrog are placed on adjacent pads in the lotus pool. Such a mystical integration of opposites is already prefigured in the bodypaint and costume of the clown in so many cultures, an amalgamation which sets together white and black, order and disorder, symmetry and asymmetry, finery and patchwork, fastidiousness and dishevelment, royal insignia and peasant attire. It is the separation and yet coincidence of Tweedledum and Tweedledee, the juxtaposition-in-unity of the baggy pants and undersize coat of a Charlie Chaplin, or the clumsied gracefulness of many a clown. It is the circus fat lady paired off with the thin man, the beautiful maiden parading with the ugly dwarf, or the graceful trapeze artist soaring above the stumbling imitations of the clown in the ring below. The mystical *coincidentia oppositorum* is symbolically achieved in the motley figure and the *punctum indifferens* of the clown-fool. His is an amorphousness and an ambiguity that represents an order of being and knowing that lies before and beyond all duality and hierarchy and intellection, in that region of freedom and innocence and playful spontaneity attained only by little children and great sages.

The Recovery of Simplicity

Parallel to this movement in Zen art is a similar collapse of the sacred and the sublime in Zen literature, almost in fact a collapse of literature at all, with the Zen preference for anecdotes and abbreviated discourse, if not simply shouts and exclamations. A comparison of the incredibly profuse productivity of the Mahāyānist literature introduced into China, as well as the extensive Theravāda *Tripitaka*, with the sparse and minimal production and use of literature in Zen is most significant. Mahāyānist sutras are even more effusive in both extensiveness and fantastic content than Mahāyānist art which certainly attempts, but is physically unable, to more than hint at the colossal proportions and stupendous numerations of the Mahāyānist visionary imagination. Mahāyānist literature opens up like an unending and inexhaustible treasurehouse of spiritual delicacies, in relation to which Zen seems to stand like a small plot of arid scrub-land to an infinity of cosmic jungles.

In place of the monumental *Mahāprajñāpāramitā Sūtra*, for example, with its 600 fascicles, Zen uses the brief *Hridaya* (heart) epitomization of the great sutra, which in its Chinese translation by Hsüan-chuang contains only 262 characters. Similarly the massiveness and luxuriance of the *Saddharma-pundarīka*, the *Vimalakīrti* and the *Avatamsaka* stand in stark contrast to the explosive abruptness of Chao-chou's (Jyōshū) '*Wu!*' or Lin-chi's (Rinzai) '*Kwatz!*' It is as if one had been invited to a sumptuous banquet table in a great hall, expecting to be gorged on a seemingly endless feast of choice meats and rare delights, only to find beneath the elegant lid of the great silver serving platter the crisp remains of a common sparrow. In fact, this is the suggestion of an anecdote told of master Fa-yen (Hōgen, 885–958) who was about to deliver a discourse to his waiting monks; but, upon ascending the platform, he heard the twittering of a swallow outside the assembly hall. Whereupon he remarked, 'What a profound discourse on Reality, and a clear exposition of the Dharma!' and descended from the platform.[29] Here the accolades of Mahāyānist piety in the *Amitābha Buddha Sūtra* are brought to a most straightforward fulfilment: 'Streams, birds and trees are all chanting Buddha and Dharma.'

The Japanese *haiku*, too, frequently associated with and used by Zen, is a fascinating instance of this same emphasis upon the common and the simple. The *haiku* is sublime in its very aversion to the sublime, and magnificent in its insistence upon being completely bereft of adornment. Clothed in the plainest and most modest garment of but seventeen syllables, and using only the most everyday elements for its subject matter, it is a poetry that only a culture with a devoted attention to the most trifling particulars, and an unusual sense of the comic, could have imagined.

> *On the temple bell*
> *Perching, sleeps*
> *The butterfly. Oh!*[30]

There are, of course, some *haikus* which are overtly humorous, as this one by Buson, or Issa's lines:

> *Yes, the young sparrows*
> *If you treat them tenderly*
> *Thank you with droppings.*[31]

But the *haiku* itself is a comic achievement. For when confronted with that which would require an infinity of words to express, it proposes to restrict itself to the very least intelligible number. And, offering itself thus as the most exquisite and purest form of poetry, it has only a beggar's display of the most mundane experiences and everyday objects, immediately accessible to anyone.

> *On a withered branch*
> *A crow has settled –*
> *Autumn nightfall.*
>
> Bashō

> *New Year's Day:*
> *Clouds dispersed, and sparrows*
> *Chattering away.*
>
> Ransetsu[32]

The *haiku* presents, as a special gift, what everybody everywhere has in his possession at all times!

There is also a sense in which – as unrelated as the two may seem – one may even speak of a collapse of the sublime and the sacred in Zen meditational practice. Again the larger Mahāyānist context must be kept in view. According to the Pure Land meditation manual, *Amitāyus Dhyāna Sūtra*, there are sixteen subjects of contemplation given by the Buddha to aid the devotees of Amitābha in visualising and ultimately attaining the glories of rebirth in his Western Paradise: the setting sun, pure water, the ground of Paradise, its jewelled trees, its merit-giving water, its jewelled palaces and heavenly music, its gem and pearl studded lotus throne, the three Holy Ones, the radiant body of Amitābha, the golden body of Avalokiteśvara, the golden body of Mahāsthāmaprāsta, Amitābha's realm of bliss, the bliss of the three Holy Ones, the superior class of rebirth in Paradise, the middle class of rebirth, and the inferior class of rebirth. In each step of the elaborate progression, the devotee is to saturate his mind with, and be elevated by, the stupendous and overwhelming images that are offered to his imagination – as in the tenth stage of contemplation, which is directed to the golden body of Avalokiteśvara (Kuan-yin):

(His) golden body reaches the height of 800,000 lacs of nayutas [millions] of yojanas [distance of a day's march], with an *uśnisa* [cranial protuberance of a Buddha], and a halo around his neck. His face, *uśnisa* and halo are each a hundred and a thousand yojanas high. Within the halo there are five hundred Nirmānakāya Buddhas who look like Śākyamuni Buddha. Each Nirmānakāya Buddha has a following of five hundred transformation Bodhisattvas together with an incalculable number of devas who serve him ... The Bodhisattva's face is of golden hue and between his eyebrows a curl of seven colours emits rays of 84,000 kinds of light. Inside each ray there is a countless number of Nirmānakāya Buddhas. Each Buddha is surrounded by an incalculable number of Transformation Bodhisattvas who serve him and reproduce at will all the transformations that fill all the worlds in the ten directions ... The Bodhisattva's palms are coloured like five hundred lacs of many hued lotus. Each finger tip has 84,000 lines as (clear as) if they had been printed thereon. Each line has 84,000 hues each of which sends out 84,000 rays of soft light which illumine everything. With these precious hands he receives and delivers living beings.[33]

The meditational practices of Zen stand in much the same kind of relationship to such contemplative luxuriance as does Zen in relation to the larger portion of such Mahāyānist literature, art and piety. Zen meditation is not meditation *on* something, let alone an infinitely expanding horizon of holy things. Nor is it contemplation attempting to soar on phantom wings to ever more grandiose and supernatural heights. The distinguishing mark of *zazen* is its utter simplicity. It does not proceed by filling the mind with an incalculable parade of images, however glorious and edifying, but by emptying the mind of all objects of attachment. It is the utter simplicity of *śūnyatā* (the Void), which is not mere emptiness, but emptiness of the clutter of objects of desire and clinging, even holy desires and a clinging to sacred things. It is an emptiness wherein lies all fullness, a fullness which comes not through filling the mind to overflowing but through emptying it, and hence opening it in the widest manner possible. Here the infinite is not reached by expanding the mind to the limits of its imagination, but by vacating it to the infinity of the Void.

The first time one is introduced to Zen meditation one searches about for something on which to contemplate. The mind furtively dances, like the monkey that it is, about the meditation hall in the frantic hope of finding something to do, some object to fix itself upon and hold to. Impatiently one waits for the show to begin, for the ritual to be performed and the sermon to be preached, for some treasury of myth and symbol to be opened up, for someone at least to say something or do something. But the show never begins. No lesson is given; no land of enchantment is offered; no edifying thought is developed; not even any background music or interlude is provided to shield one from the silence. Nothing happens. One is confronted only with bare walls, the minimum of ritual, and the silence of emptiness, interrupted only by the awakening and alerting blows of the *keisaku*.

This is not, however, a substitution of a mere nothingness for the bewildering profuseness of Pure Land contemplation. *Śūnyatā* is not a quantitative but a qualitative emptiness. The possibility of such a misunderstanding is provided with a typically Zen corrective in K'uo-an's (Kakuan, 12th century) meditational drawings, with commentary, of the Ten Bulls, based on the earlier Taoist Eight Bulls. The Taoist sequence had symbolised the culmination of the search for Truth and Reality by an empty frame, representing the Nothingness beyond both object (bull) and self (man). K'uo-an, however, added two more scenes which rescued the progression from what might have been construed as a termination in the dead end of a barren nothingness. His ninth scene, 'Reaching the Source,' depicts a tree, a bird, and a stream with fish; while the tenth, that of 'In the World,' depicts a monk approaching a child, and 'mingling with the people of the world.' (See plate 10.) Another line of K'uo-an's commentary reads, 'I go to the market place with my wine bottle and return home with my staff.'

This escape from a sterile, if not abstract, emptiness is what is also so clearly seen in the popular figure of Pu-tai, dancing or playing with the village children – of which K'uo-an's tenth scene is reminiscent. Insofar as pictures are appropriate at all, the picture which best symbolises the Zen experience of emptiness, and the context of that experience, is not the empty frame, but the ordinary world of trees and birds and fish, the world of shops and wine bottles and walking-sticks, seen now through, and in, the experience of *sūnyatā*. As Shan-neng, a Zen master of the Southern Sung period, put it: 'We must not cling to the wind and moon of the day and ignore the eternal Void; neither should we cling to the eternal Void and give no attention to the wind and moon of the day.'[34]

Like the world of the comic spirit and perspective, which also has its way of returning everything to the Source and to the World, Zen brings everything back down, not only from a mythic otherworldliness, but from a vacuous emptiness, down to the very humble and unpretentious level of mingling with people, going to the market place, and returning home. As Chia-shan (Kyōzan, d. 881) once remarked to his disciples: 'You should perceive this old monk in the tips of the grass, and recognise the son of heaven in a crowded market.'[35] The point is similarly expressed as the achievement of the fifth and highest stage in Tung-shan Shou-ch'u's (Tōzan Susho, 10th century) schematised path of enlightenment:

> Lo, he has arrived at supreme unity!
> Beyond the 'is' and the 'is not,'
> Who dares to follow the rhymes of his poetry?
> Let others aspire to the extraordinary!
> He is happy to return home and sit amidst ashes.[36]

As Alan Watts has suggested, 'according to Zen, the reason why our quest for some ultimate reality is so difficult is that we are looking in obscure places for what is out in broad daylight.'[37] What is needed is not a closing of the eyes, or some dazzling psychedelic vision, but their opening to the reality that stands plainly and nakedly before us and within us. The only requirement is the very difficult, and yet perfectly simple and natural, one of seeing things as they are apart from the filter of categories, without the interposition of value judgments or thoughts of possession and use – without even the enhancement of some symbolic aura or mythic colouration. It is to see the world and the self in that isness or suchness, that emptiness, which lies behind and beyond all words, all estimations of value and purpose, all symbols and myths. For these only serve to cloak reality in the very act of attempting to mediate and clarify it. Thus a novice once asked master Chao-chou (Jyōshū), thinking to obtain some lofty teaching or profound discourse: 'I have just entered the brotherhood and am anxious to learn the first principle of Zen. Will you please teach it to me?' Chao-chou responded, 'Have you eaten your supper?' The novice replied, 'I have.' 'Then go wash your bowl!'[38]

It must be said, nevertheless, in all fairness, that the incredibly sublime visions of so much of Mahāyānist art, literature and meditation, if not taken literally but as highly symbolic profusions of imagery, may be seen to be pointing, in their own fantastic and allegorical way, to many of the same insights as are to be found in Zen. As Suzuki points out, such motifs as the intricate interrelatedness of all things, the interpenetration of the most infinitesimal particle and the totality, the profound sense of inscrutable mystery, and the realisation of the presence of the whole in its meanest part, are already there in the Mahāyānist tradition, but now intuited by Zen in the most plain, straightforward and no-nonsense manner.[39] They are reached in Zen, not through a fabulous display of fantasy which runs the risk of simply swelling the imagination and boggling the mind, but through a complete elimination of all marvels and embellishments in an effort to move directly to the heart of the manner: as in the laying aside of the 600 fascicles of the *Mahāprajñāpāramitā Sūtra* for a concentration upon the bare 262 characters of the *Hridaya* (heart) of the sutra, or the reduction of the entire scriptural corpus, as it were, to a single '*Kwatz!*'

There is a definite dialectical relationship here between the two Buddhist poles represented by Amidism and Ch'an of the sublime and the common-mundane, the fantastic and the ordinary, the infinitely complex and esoteric and the utterly simple and obvious. The Zen emphasis does not stand alone; rather it has meaning in the larger context of the Great Vehicle of Mahāyāna. The very acts of profanation and inversion involve an element of relationship and interdependence. Any impact derives in part from the force of its counterpart, and exists relative to it, just as the point of a joke cannot be made unless at least a modicum of its opposite (seriousness and rationality) precedes it. Like the opposition and yet harmony of the *yin* and the *yang* in relation to the Tao, the sublime and the simple are relative perspectives which counterbalance and complement each other, which are in tension and yet in harmony, and whose harmony moves into that higher harmony that is the Tao or the Dharmakāya itself. Both in their own ways point toward the ultimate mystery of being, the one by the overpowering majesty of its images, the other by the amazing simplicity, the incredible poverty, of its forms.

Notes

1. George Santayana, *The Sense of Beauty* (New York: Scribners, 1896), page 188.
2. Kenji Toda, *Japanese Scroll Paintings* (Chicago: University of Chicago Press, 1935), pages 53 ff.
3. Similarly in 1916, when two statues in the Tōshōdaiji temple were removed for repairs, playful sketches were discovered on the stands underneath. Dating from the 8th century, they included a motley array of not-particularly-divine figures: horses, monkeys, birds, rabbits, frogs and a mantis. *Ibid.*, pages 49–50.
4. Sirén, **IV**, 11.
5. Brief descriptions of the wall paintings found in Buddhist temples and monasteries in China prior to the destruction of many of them in 845–9 are to be found in the *Li-tai-ming-hua-chi*. Cf. Acker, pages 254–377.
6. See T. Naito, *The Wall Paintings of Hōryūji*, translated by W. R. B. Acker and B. Rowland (Baltimore: Waverly, 1943).
7. D. T. Suzuki, *Zen and Japanese Buddhism*, 4th edition (Tokyo: Japanese Tourist Bureau, 1965), page 35.
8. *Essays in the Philosophy of Art* (Bloomington: Indiana University Press, 1946), pages 81–2.
9. Cf. Helen B. Chapin, 'Three Early Portraits of Bodhidharma,' *Archives of the Chinese Art Society of America*, **I** (1945–6), pages 66–97.
10. Suzuki, *Japanese Culture*, page 379.
11. Charles Luk, *Secrets of Chinese Meditation* (London: Rider, 1964), pages 94–5.
12. Suzuki, **III**, 82.
13. Sirén, **V**, 69.
14. Suzuki, **III**, 107.
15. Naito, pages 59 ff.
16. Suzuki, **III**, 372.
17. Cf. Suzuki, *Japanese Culture*, page 348.
18. Osvald Sirén, *The Chinese and the Art of Painting* (Peiping, 1936), page 91.
19. Munsterberg, page 90.
20. Hu Shih, 'The Development of Zen Buddhism in China,' *The Chinese Social and Political Science Review*, **XV** (April, 1932), pages 481–2.
21. Thomas Merton, *The Way of Chuang-tzu* (New York: New Directions, 1965), page 16.

22. Yutang, *My People*, page 89.
23. From the *Hsüan-ho-hua-p'u* (1120) and the *Li-tai-ming-hua-chi* (847).
24. Teng-chu'un's *Hua-chi* (1167) seems to suggest a Ch'an monk, while in the *Hsüan-ho-hua-p'u* this advice was given by a Taoist.
25. Cf. Agnes Meyer, *Chinese Painting, as Reflected in the Thought and Art of Li Lung-mien* (New York: Duffield, 1923), pages 56–8.
26. Sirén, **II**, 55.
27. Luk, **II**, 74.
28. Wu, page 89.
29. *Ibid.*, page 230.
30. Suzuki, *Japanese Culture*, page 248.
31. Blyth, *Haiku*, **II**, 235.
32. Henderson, pages 18, 53.
33. Luk, *Secrets*, pages 95–6.
34. Wu, page 247.
35. Luk, **II**, 191.
36. Wu, page 182.
37. Nancy Wilson Ross, editor, *The World of Zen* (New York: Random House, 1960), page 123.
38. No author, *Zen Buddhism* (Mt. Vernon: Peter Pauper, 1959), page 33.
39. Suzuki, **III**, 78–95.

FOUR   *The Celebration of the Commonplace*

Drinking tea, eating rice,
Passing time as it comes;
Looking down at the stream,
Looking up at the mountain . . .
PAO-TZU

It is commonly asserted that the Chinese and Japanese are basically a non-religious people, at least as judged by Western or Indian standards. Certainly there is an emphasis upon the pragmatic, the human, the everyday and the this-worldly, and a relative lack of interest in metaphysical speculation, theological formulation, mythological vision and devotional liturgy. Certainly also the term *aesthetics* often seems more appropriate than the term *religion*, and the finest expressions of the Oriental spirit culminate in art and poetry rather than in myth and ritual or religious philosophy. If emphasis is laid, however, upon a sensitivity to ultimate mystery, where religion and art necessarily meet, that fundamental level of experience which lies behind and within all experience, even the most ordinary and commonplace, and in which the inexhaustible mystery of being manifests itself to human consciousness, then the Chinese and Japanese in their profound appreciation of this *mysterium* in poetry and painting are as religious as any.

What is particularly intriguing, in fact, is that whereas many peoples tend to locate this experience in certain unusual, if not 'supernatural' moments and circumstances out of which it is evoked, the Oriental focus is upon mystery in the most obvious, ordinary, mundane – the most natural – situations of life. In the words of the Ch'an master, Yüan-wu (Engo), 'One particle of dust is raised, and the great earth lies therein; one flower blooms, and the universe rises with it.'[1]

Everyday-mindedness

The terms used by Yüan-wu derive from a Mahāyānist text, the *Gandavyūka*, in which the wondrous power of the Buddha is seen as manifest in his ability to interpenetrate all phenomena, so that the tiniest particle contains the entirety of the whole:

> All this is because he has the miraculous power of transforming his one body and making it pervade the entire universe . . . It is because he has the miraculous power of manifesting all the images of the Dharmadhāta within one single particle of dust; it is because he has the miraculous power of revealing all the Buddhas of the past with their successive doings within a single pore of his skin.[2]

Though it is to this theme that Yüan-wu alludes, his use of it is quite different. It is as different as the search for the miraculous beyond the world of the everyday in some ethereal realm of preternatural transformations, and the realisation of the miraculousness that is to be found in the everyday world itself, whether in a single particle of dust or a single pore of skin. The colossal world of the Indian *Gandavyūka* has been stood on its head. It is not a matter of the Buddha engaged in miraculous metamorphoses, manifesting the entirety of the Buddha-world in a single particle of dust. It is the single particle of dust which contains in itself that holy miracle and sublime secret and sacred being of the whole. The one wild flower, unnoticed by the wayside, opens out upon and is inseparable from, the entire universe.

When master Chi-ch'en was asked what was meant by the 'way upward' commonly spoken of in the Zen tradition, he responded by saying, 'You will hit it by descending lower.'[3] It is this ascent by means of descent, this discovery of the sublime in the commonplace, this revelation of the totality in the slightest particular, that is so characteristic of Zen. Surely the celebrated Chinese matter-of-factness and practicality is evident here, bringing a refreshing clearheadedness and directness and simplicity to the Mahāyānist tradition. But just as surely the dimension of wonder and mystery is present as well, though in its own inverted, down-to-earth manner. As Suzuki has insisted, 'In spite of its matter-of-factness, there is an air of mystery and spirituality in Zen, which was later on developed into a form of nature-mysticism. Hu Shih* ... thinks Zen is the revolt of Chinese psychology against abstruse Buddhist metaphysics. But the fact is that it is not a revolt but a deep appreciation. Only the appreciation could not be expressed in any other way than in the Chinese way.'[4]

The distinctiveness in this Chinese (and Zen) outlook lies in its peculiar combination of accepting the concrete 'suchness' (*tathatā*) of the mundane particular, while at the same time realising the inexhaustible significance and mystery in the most commonplace object or situation. And in this is further reason why the comic spirit, which is so much at home in the this-worldly, and takes such delight in inversions and surprises, is so much at home in Zen, and why in Zen the relationship between mystery, comedy and the earthy and everyday is so clearly articulated.

The master clown Grock in his autobiography, *Life's A Lark*, saw the special genius of his occupation that of 'transforming the little, everyday annoyances, not only overcoming, but actually *transforming* them into something strange and terrific.' It is 'the power to extract mirth for millions out of nothing and less than nothing: a wig, a stick of grease paint, a child's fiddle, a chair without a seat.'[5] This is also a part of the special genius of Zen, the difference being that such a transformation-power presupposes that there is already something strange and terrific about the little everyday objects and trifling events which is usually missed because of their familiarity or their apparent triviality. One looks for a miracle in the fantastic transformations of the Bodhisattva, when it is right there in the speck of dust, or the child's toy. When Ch'u-hui first became abbot, he was asked by a resident monk, 'I

*See above, page 67.

hear that when Śākyamuni began his public life, golden lotus sprang from the earth. Today, at the inauguration of Your Reverence, what auspicious sign may we expect?' The new abbot replied, 'I have just swept away the snow before the gate!'[6] Or one may cite Yün-mēn who, on picking up a piece of firewood which his monks had just gathered, tossed it on the ground before them with the remark: 'The whole *Tripitaka* expounds only this thing!'[7]

It is this perception of the uncommon commonplaceness of things that underlies much of the comic iconoclasm in Zen, and its collapsing of the categories of the sacred and the sublime. Again and again the point is stressed in Zen literature, art and life. Ch'ang-ch'ing (Chōkei, 854–932) asked: 'What is the language of the Tathāgata [the Buddha]?' Pao-fu (Hofuku, d. 928) replied, 'Come, have a cup of tea!'[8] Or Yün-mēn when asked to give some extraordinary statement for the enlightenment of his monks, replied in the most ordinary terms: 'Pulling a plough in the morning, and carrying a rake home in the evening.'[9] As Suzuki repeatedly maintained: 'Wherever the spirit of Zen moves, everything that comes in touch with it acquires something of mystery about it. The oil jar carried by T'ou-tzū emits an ineffable glow; the ladle in the hand of Hsüeh-fēng is incalculably more than a wooden stick; the straw sandal on the head of Chao-chou is worth sharing a corner in the temple treasure house.'[10]

In concert with this is the persistent Zen debunking of the religious search for the exotic and the supranormal, as if this were the locus of the sacred and the true seat of Buddha and Dharma. Bankei (1622–93), for instance, was once interrupted during a sermon by a zealous Shin-shū priest. 'The founder of our sect,' boasted the priest, 'has such miraculous powers that he held a brush in his hand on one bank of the river, his attendant held up a paper on the other bank, and the teacher wrote the holy name of Amida through the air. Can you do such a wonderful thing?' Bankei replied simply, 'Perhaps your fox can perform that trick; but that is not the manner of Zen. My miracle is that when I feel hungry I eat, and when I feel thirsty

I drink.'[11] A similar tale is told of Huang-po (Ōbaku, 9th century) who, while walking with another monk, came to a river. As Huang-po stood wondering how to get across, the other monk walked across the river without even getting his feet wet. When Huang-po saw this he exclaimed, 'Oh, I didn't know he could do this; otherwise I should have pushed him right down to the bottom of the river.'[12] The same emphasis is given in one of the more popular *kōans*, which plays upon the legend of the wondrous visitations of Niu-t'ou that ceased after his Zen awakening: 'How was it that before Niu-t'ou had met the Fourth Patriarch, the birds used to flock. to him with flowers in their beaks, while after his enlighten- ment the prodigy ceased?'[13] Yün-mēn is characteristically far less circumspect about the matter. He once related the legend to his monks, according to which the Buddha at his birth pointed toward heaven with one hand and the earth with the other, and taking seven steps forward looked toward the four quarters of the earth, exclaiming: 'Above and beneath heaven, I alone am the Honoured One.' Yün-mēn then de- clared: 'If I had seen him at the time, I would have cut him down with my staff, and given his flesh to dogs to eat, so that peace could prevail over all the world.'[14]

Many such Zen stories reflect the same suspicion and hum- orous scepticism of the goggling delight in the fabulous that is the perennial soil for man's strange fascination for wizards and magicians, ghosts and goblins, witches and demons. For in excess such fascination provides too great a diversion from the principal human tasks and dilemmas, if not a camouflage of the real issues at hand, as well as a devaluation of what then be- come, by contrast, the commonplaces of human experience. In this reaction lies a profound sense of the ambiguity of the sacred which, though it may be seen as that which gives meaning and worth to the profane sphere over against which it sets itself apart, yet at the same time it may by its very sep- arateness and elevation tend to empty the profane sphere of significance and value. In the claim that this sacred reality is the infinite source and repository of all power and worth lies the apparent negation of the possibility for any intrinsic power and worth in things themselves. As a result, offering itself as the ultimate basis of salvation, it may instead either elicit a defiant emptying of the heavens and repudiation of all sacrality in favour of secularity, or become the place of evasion and retreat, a refuge from reality rather than a response to it.

In either case what is missed is the suchness and wondrousness of things in themselves, however commonplace and seemingly inconsequential. As one master exclaimed, 'The beauty of a mountain is that it is so much like a mountain, and of water that it is so much like water.' This is the acceptance and celebration of things as they are: beyond and before all thought of useful and useless, subject and object, mine and not-mine, good and bad, holy and unholy, marvellous and ordinary. It is the suchness of the flower – even the lotus flower – which is not first of all a sign or symbol that stands for something else, and that points away from itself to some other, more important, more sacred and more desirable something. The flower is a flower. That is its meaning, its purpose, its goodness and its mystery. The flower points primarily to its flowerness, indeed to the particular flowerness of that particular flower. A flower *means* a flower. What greater value and importance and holiness and miraculousness can it have than this? If its function is simply to point away from itself, or to be caught up in some other meaning, instead of its gaining in worth and significance, it is actually emptied of its own meaning and being in order to serve in this depreciating capacity of 'meaning' something else. Instead of the Buddha holding up the lotus flower (or, in the case of the wordless sermon on Vulture Peak, the sandalwood flower), the lotus flower must then hold up the Buddha.

It was Ch'ing-yüan (Seigin, d. 740) who announced: 'Before I underwent (Ch'an) training, I saw mountains as mountains, and rivers as rivers. After I had called on enlightened persons, I managed to enter (Ch'an) and saw mountains were not mountains, and rivers were not rivers. Now that I have stopped (my false discriminating thought), I see that mountains are mountains and rivers are rivers, as before.'[15] Nan-chu'an's (Nansen, 748–834) answer to the question, 'What is the Tao?' is most revealing of the Zen mind in this. 'Your everyday mind is the Tao.' Here 'everyday mind' (*p'ing-ch'ang hsin*) points to nothing esoteric or supernatural or abnormal, no fantastic psychic state or ecstatic trance, nor any exalted gnosis available only to some inner circle of privileged elite. It is of course the everyday mind seen in a different light, the uncommon light of *satori*. But Zen does not dwell in the ivory tower of uncanny religious experience; it lives in the world of the everyday. Therefore, though in relation to the unenlightened it may be an extraordinary way of perceiving things, from the Zen standpoint it is perfectly ordinary; for it is perceiving things in a completely natural way through one's 'original mind.'

This relationship between suchness, mystery and the comic-mundane was most simply, yet profoundly, expressed in the exclamation of P'ang Chü-shih (Hō-koji, 8th century):

> *How wondrous this, how mysterious!*
> *I carry fuel, I draw water.*[16]

The immediate inclination in interpreting these lines is to see in them a very serious and sobering realisation of the awesome mystery that interpenetrates even the most menial activity, such as carrying fuel and drawing water, and a startling awareness of the 'isness' of things, quite apart from judgments of meaning, value and utility. And this is certainly there. Yet something else is there too; and that is the comic perception of suchness and mystery, the response of laughter to the sudden discernment of the most commonplace things in a new light, the surprised amazement over the wondrousness of the simplest task and the humblest of elements.

Once when all the monks attached to master Tai-chu (Daishu, d. 814) were engaged in tilling their farm, there was one monk who, upon hearing the dinner drum, at once raised his spade and gave out a hearty laugh and went off. Tai-chu remarked: 'What an intelligent fellow! This is the way to enter the Kuan-yin gate of truth.' When he returned to the monastery, he sent for the monk and inquired, 'What was the truth you saw awhile ago when you heard the drum?' Answered the monk, 'Nothing much, master. As I heard the dinner drum go, I went back and had my meal.' This time it was the master who gave out a hearty laugh.[17] This immediate intuition of the sacred suchness of even so profane a matter as dinner and its summons has itself a comic dimension, and is often accompanied by laughter. For laughter, too, is a 'breaking through the intellectual barrier; at the moment of laughing something is understood; it needs no proof of itself.'[18] The moment of insight, which abruptly perceives with unshrouded clarity things-in-themselves, and at the same time with equal clarity the wondrousness of their inscrutable mystery, is marked as appropriately by laughter as by hushed reverence. Indeed such laughter is itself a form of reverence; it is the laughter of acceptance, and appreciation and wonder.

This is made explicit in Tsu-yüan's (Sogen, 13th century) description of the moment and occasion of his enlightenment: 'Looking up to the sky I laughed loudly, "Oh, how great is the Dharmakāya [the most exalted of the three "bodies" of the Buddha, hence the fundamental level of reality]! Oh, how great and immense for evermore!" Thence my joy knew no bounds.'[19] It is this moment, however trifling the occasion, toward which much of Zen attempts to lead, or to give expression to, a moment in which the sublime and the ridiculous, the monumental and trivial, seriousness and laughter, meet in an experience which contains them both in a joyful acceptance and celebration of existence.

That Playfulness That Cannot Be Netted

Of similar significance is the use of ambiguity and indefiniteness in Zen and Zen art. For ambiguity is a part of the province of comedy, made most explicit in the double-meanings of puns and plays upon words, but also in the rather amorphous habit of the clown and fool, their blurring of distinctions and conventional discriminations, and the unpredictability of their behaviour. Reality cannot be pinned down, netted, boxed or frozen. In this lies the perennial threat posed by the comic in relation to the sacred, to reason and order, to 'clear and distinct ideas,' to the crispness of all boundaries and delineations. For the comic jest or jester does not simply profane Beauty, Truth, Goodness and Holiness, but rather muddies them, places their purity and preciseness somewhat in doubt, and calls them to a vague, chartless no-man's land between competing categories and forces. This ambiguity itself heralds that 'wondrous playfulness' that moves within all phenomena, disturbing all the labelled drawers of the mind, emptying them and sporting with their contents, returning both form and content to the inexhaustible source of their being.

In Zen painting the employment of ambiguity and indefiniteness is especially apparent in the combined focus upon the suchness (*tathatā*) of the concrete image and the Void (*śūnyatā*) that is in and beyond that image. On both counts Zen art insists on being imprecise and incomplete. This is in marked contrast with Indian art which moves away from the concrete actuality in favour of the stylised purity of an ideal form, and which avoids empty space in favour of a 'finished' composition or profusely sculptured façade. Similarly in traditional Western art there often appears to be a horror of the Void, and consequently an anxious concern to fill every point in the canvas or fresco with something, if only background and colouration. It is as if, as in classical Western physics, nature is supposed to abhor a vacuum, or, as in Western philosophy and theology, Nothingness implies the threatening, nihilating, chaotic abyss: the bottomless pit over which created things are precariously suspended. But in Zen, as in Taoism and Buddhism generally, formlessness is seen in very positive, dynamic, creative terms, and emptiness is the most appropriate designation for the ultimate reality and basic truth of all things.

In Indian Buddhism, artistic representation is involved in the paradox of attempting to point toward this emptiness by means of fullness, the Void by means of the All. For in the Indian tradition, much as in the classical Western tradition, the infinity and incomprehensibility and holy mystery at the root of all things is best suggested by means of a seemingly endless multiplicity of figures and a riot of detail, a representation of infinity by what appears to be a literal infinity of forms, as reflected in both Indian art and architectural adornment. This tradition is continued in the richness and grandeur of the Mahāyānist art and literature that invades China. But in Zen art, and that of the Sung dynasty contemporaneous with its beginnings, these concerns are arrived at in an opposite way: intimations of infinity and transcendence, of sublimity and mystery, are achieved through a creative use of empty space and indefiniteness of form.

This Oriental perception of the profundity of empty space was most amenable to a suggestion of the Void, a Void which is not simply blank space, or unfinished space, or waste space, and not simply nothing at all, but in its own way a powerful, mysterious, blissful nothingness, full of potentiality and life. It is not merely the absence of forms or of light, nor the negation of these, but the presence of all vitality, purity, simplicity, immensity. As Huang-po (Ōbaku) said of emptiness: 'All these phenomena are intrinsically void, and yet this Mind with which they are identical is no mere nothingness. By this I mean that it does exist, but in a way too marvellous for us to comprehend. It is an existence which is no existence, a non-existence which is nevertheless existence. So this true Void does in some marvellous way "exist."' [20]

The full employment of this occurs in Southern Sung (1126–1279) painting in conjunction with the movement away from solidity of representation to a more suggestive sketching of bare outlines and minimal features (the *p'o-mo* manner). By 'emptying' the forms of solidity and elaborate detail, and by a creative use of empty space, the artist is simultaneously able to capture both the suchness of the object beneath all the superimposed categories of rationality, value and utility, and the inexhaustible mystery within the object, the mystery of the Void. The *ch'i* (spirit), therefore, that informs the composition throughout is that of grasping both the transparent suchness, yet infinite elusiveness of things. It is an artistry that, by means of concrete but indefinite imagery, reveals the lucid yet unfathomable character of existence, and its inexpressibility except in ambiguously suggestive terms, which therefore both disclose and cloak its reality. As Lytton Strachey phrased it, in contrasting Greek and Chinese art and poetry: 'Greek art is ... the most finished in the world; it is forever seeking to express itself completely and finally. (Chinese art) aims at producing an impression which, so far from being final, must be merely the prelude to a long series of visions and of feelings. It hints at wonders; and the revelation it at last gives us is never a complete one; it is clothed in the indefinability of our subtlest thoughts.'[21]

The poetic ideal of *yūgen* (depth or mystery) developed in Japanese poetry in the 12th century is similarly achieved by a certain imprecision or vague intimation in language and imagery, or by the ambiguity of the language itself which offers a pool of meaning, rather than a unilinear suggestion. This is also apparent in many of the later *haikus* which on the one hand are quite precise in their reference to the most everyday objects and events, and in their restriction to seventeen scrupulously chosen syllables. Yet at the same time they contain an utter simplicity and absolute minimum of expression that can only begin to hint in the direction of experiences which words-unending could never grasp or exhaust. The same achievement is visible in the *Noh* plays, with their use of a plain stage, a modicum of props, obscure language and symbolic gestures. They 'don't come right out and say what they're after,' as an unsympathetic tourist might well remark. It is not, however, just that something is left for the imagination, and consequently for the creativity and participation of the observer – the point customarily made of the matter – but that nothing, however simple and commonplace, can be completely imaged or contained or exhausted at the rational and phenomenal level. Art, therefore, like life, must conceal its point as much as it reveals it, as in the artful artlessness of the Tea Ceremony.

This is also, interestingly, at the very heart of comedy which in an analogous manner relies upon the double meanings of words, gestures and situations – their ambiguity – for triggering laughter. The comic spirit and perspective is, thus, particularly suited to effecting the kind of deeper realisation of the inner nature of things which Zen and Zen art is after. As a result, the sudden perception of this element of ambiguity, and of the underlying suchness and mystery of things, even the most ordinary and trivial, is often expressed by laughter – as Blyth has termed it, 'the laughter of surprised approval.'[22] This is quaintly illustrated in the Zen tale of Yao-shan (Yakusan, 758–834) who had climbed the mountain near his monastery for a walk. When he saw the moon suddenly appear from behind the clouds, he laughed heartily, so much so that his laugh echoed for ninety *li* east of the monastery. In the morning the villagers inquired of one another as to who was laughing so raucously in the middle of the night, disturbing everyone's sleep. And finding that it was not the laughter of any of the villagers, they concluded (suggesting that Yao-shan had a reputation for this type of behaviour): 'Last night the master gave us the greatest laugh of his life at the top of the mountain.'[23]

One of the functions of the comic is to call attention to the element of ambiguity in all things, an ambiguity which admits of different interpretations and perceptions, none of which should be absolutised or taken with absolute seriousness. Here comedy is a reminder of the finiteness and fallibility of all individual perspectives. Comedy also points to a further ambiguity, simply by being comedy, and that is the ambiguity of the sacred and the comic, or of the sublime and the ridiculous, an ambiguity in which the same concern can be treated as sacred and sublime and therefore serious, and yet comic and therefore humorous. Though the comic perspective is commonly seen as extraneous, if not inimical, to the inner soul of spiritual awakening and illumination, it has its own ontological and epistemological significance. So that, as in the case of Yao-shan, the response of awe upon seeing the moon and the response of laughter are both appropriate responses, and both reveal something about man and the nature of reality. Both point in their own way to the dimension of such-ness and mystery beyond the matter-of-fact level of perception (i.e., the mere noticing of the moon), and beyond the distorted seeing of the discriminating-mind. And the sudden realisation of this is as amusing as it is sobering, as filled with playfulness as with earnestness, even though the heavy-handedness and soberness of most religion tends to channel this realisation in the latter direction.

Is reality, after all, really serious, as we so habitually suppose, and not humorous? Is the ponderous movement of the planets, or the darting of little fishes, actually to be construed as a serious motion? And what of Kikaku's

> Tree frog, clinging
> To a banana leaf,
> And swinging, swinging.

Or what is one to do with Issa's

> Giant firefly:
> That way, this way, that way, this –
> And it passes by.[24]

Does not their being and doing lie beyond the distinction between seriousness and laughter, such that to approach them only seriously, and to see them only in their 'seriousness,' is a distortion of the first order? Is this great drama not also as great a comedy? And is this sober work not also a marvellous form of play, a prodigious frolicking of whirling galaxies and whirling atoms and whirling whirligigs?

On the one hand it may be said that comedy, like beauty, is in the eye of the beholder, and therefore that seeing things in comic perspective is a matter of the way in which the world appears, rather than a quality intrinsic to things themselves. Yet to be satisfied with this subjectivist statement of the situation (and its separation of subject and object) is often to ignore the alternative presuppositions which may unconsciously substitute themselves – namely, that reality is fundamentally 'serious' or 'dramatic' or 'at work.' In this way the denial of any epistemological and ontological appropriateness to the images and metaphors related to the comic very easily becomes an unexamined confirmation of another set of basic images and metaphors. From the Zen standpoint, one must someway cut through, not only such onesidedness, but the distinction between sides, whether subjective versus objective, dramatic versus comic, or work versus play. Wu-mēn (Mumon), for example, in a verse written upon his *satori*, captures in a higher unity all these dimensions:

> *From the blue sky, the sun glowing white – a peal of thunder!*
> *All living things on earth open their eyes widely;*
> *Multiplicities endless uniformly bow their heads in respect;*
> *Lo and behold, Mt. Sumeru is off its base folk-dancing merrily!*[25]

Absurdity in the Comic Mode

Twentieth-century man has been introduced to a sense of the absurd with a vengeance that is in no small measure the result of the failure of, and inevitable reaction to, an overweening effort to bring all things under the dominion of human reason, progress and control. Consequently our experiences of irrationality, meaninglessness and chaos are deeply tragic. Yet absurdity is also at the heart of *comic* awareness. It is the abrupt peception of absurdity that triggers laughter (the comic twist). Humour plays with nonsense and foolishness. Joking delights in the irrational. Clowns incarnate confusions and contradictions. And comedy, unlike drama, or any serious literary structure, refuses to abide by the same requirement to make sense, to conform to a plot, or to uphold the canons of law and order. Each of these forms has, to be sure, a certain logic of its own. But it is a logic based upon absurdity, and employing almost every conceivable violation of the commonly accepted categories of rationality, value, purpose, goodness, beauty and holiness. Yet in this comic perception of absurdity lies the potential for a deeper level of insight into the element of absurdity in all things, even the most obvious and assured, and for a deeper level of acceptance and celebration of things in spite of their final recalcitrance to human patterns and designs.

There is, of course, a laughter of cynicism and despair which shouts out some last gesture of futility in the darkness – an heroic, perhaps, but nevertheless bitter flourish in the face of the bankruptcy of foundering systems. Yet this is not the comic spirit, which also deals with absurdity (and rationality as well), but does so more freely. The comic spirit does not come into being at the end of the rope, or upon the loss of all bearings, which would make of it a grimace, or a hollow guffaw. It is something far more positive and basic, buoyant, and fuller of laughter. In fact, in large part, the tragedies and absurdities of our time – and the death of all but a grotesque laughter which they bring – are the consequence of a prior refusal to give due recognition and place to the comic spirit.

The problem of absurdity has become particularly acute in the West – e.g., the existentialism of Sartre, the 'theatre of the absurd' and the work of various playwrights from Chekhov to Ionesco, Robbe-Grillet, Beckett and Albee. This is partly because of an anxious and increasingly desperate attempt within the history of Western theologies and ideologies to decipher a substratum of meaning, purpose and destiny in life. With the shattering of so noble a presumption we are shocked, disillusioned, dismayed. But this is also because of an all-pervasive seriousness about the attempt, and a failure to cultivate laughter in relation to the stubborn refusal of things to fit into the neat patterns of rationality and order devised for them. It is the failure to discover laughter, both in absurdity and the attempted overcoming of absurdity, and to perceive a dimension of playfulness, as it were, in all things which transcends the oppositions between meaning and meaninglessness, purpose and purposelessness, value and valuelessness.

It is the absence of this attempt, so characteristic of Western intellectual history, to press existence for reason and purpose – or conversely to despair over absurdity and the tragic absence of the good, the true and the beautiful in everything – that has enabled the Chinese and Japanese generally to have a singular acceptance of life as it is, to see through to the suchness and mystery of things beyond the schemas of intellection and value judgment, beyond the towering hierarchies and grand systems, and to do so with grace and good humour. In this earthiness, and its devotion to the simplest particulars of life – quite apart from any cumbersome intellectual structures which are supposed to give them a 'place' and to guarantee their worth, but which unfortunately have the bad habit of suffering periodic collapses – lies that uncommon wisdom, that fine sense of the comic, and that affirmation of things in themselves, which is crystallised in Zen.

There is, after all, an element of absurdity in even the most accepted truths and established facts and conventions, as in the experience of using a familiar word that suddenly looks or sounds funny, that suddenly is absurd, like all words. This is one of the things which comedy – and Zen – so well perceives. Even that which makes most sense, which is beyond doubt, which is the common knowledge of us all, suddenly seems to make no sense at all, to defy rationality, to be completely dubious and ambiguous, and shrouded in profound mystery. As Santayana put it, 'Existence ... is comic inherently ... This world is contingency and absurdity incarnate, the oddest of possibilities masquerading momentarily as fact.'[26] On the one hand this is the suchness of things, a perception lying beyond their utility, their value, their mental classification, as well as their sense, purpose and meaning. Things are seen perfectly clearly beyond the filter of categories and in an unusually fresh and lucid light. On the other hand this suchness of things is at the same time a perception of their inexhaustible mystery – not in the sense of the 'mystery story' which will be solved on the final page of the detective's investigation, and therefore no longer constitute a mystery, but in the sense of an ultimate mystery that is to be found in even the most obvious and ordinary areas of experience where no particular problem appears at all, and where no absurdity is immediately apparent.

ILLUSTRATIONS

1 Han-shan and Shih-tē YEN-HUI

2 The three laughing monks of Hu-hsi   SOGA SHŌHAKU

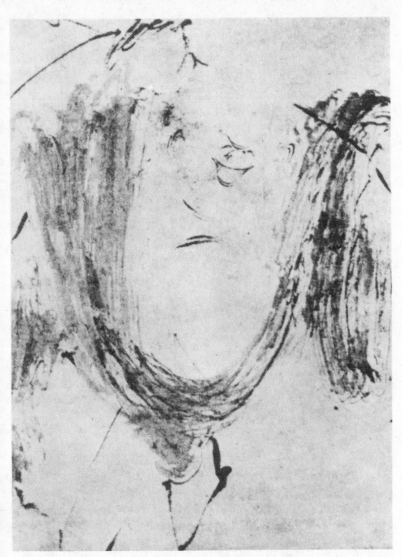

3 Pu-tai dancing LIANG-K'AI

4 Bodhidharma MATABEI

5 The Bullfrog Buddha · Toba-sōjō. *From the Animal Scroll Scenes (chōjū-giga)*

6 Meditating frog SENGAI

'If by practising zazen
One becomes a
Buddha ....'

7 Hui-nēng tearing up the sutras   LIANG-K'AI

8 Tan-hsia burning the Buddha-image SENGAI

9 Self-portrait HAKUIN

10 Entering the city with bliss-bestowing hands SHUBUN, *after
K'uo-an's Tenth Cow-herding picture*

His thatched cottage gate is closed; and even the wisest know him not. No glimpses of his inner life are to be caught; for he goes on his own way without following the steps of the ancient sages. Carrying a gourd he goes out into the market; leaning against a staff he comes home. He is found in company with winebibbers and butchers. He and they are all converted into Buddhas.

> *Bare chested and barefooted, he comes out into the market place;*
> *Daubed with mud and ashes, how broadly he smiles!*
> *There is no need for the miraculous power of the gods;*
> *For he touches, and lo! the dead trees are in full bloom!*
> K'UO-AN

If the use of the term 'absurdity' is acceptable in Zen as a symbol of the inadequacy and final frustration of reason, and of the nonsensical methods employed to effect a leap beyond intellection, it is not a category implying despair or alienation or anxiety as in Western existentialism. If anything, it is a perception of absurdity that precipitates laughter, not despair, and that moves beyond alienation and anxiety into a joyful wonder. It does not arise out of the loss of a sense of meaning in life. No great light has failed; no sacred vision has been lost or become impossible. Indeed enlightenment has occurred, and everything has been gained. It is not the dark abyss of infinite nothingness that has been entered, but that blissful, wondrous emptiness wherein lies all fullness. And it is in no way anxious or estranged, or condemned to an alienated consciousness; but is free in that freedom where inner harmony and well-being are not fettered to the attempt at coercing and possessing the world, or turning it into a problem.

The Zen appreciation and employment of absurdity is also not to be confused with a retreat into a kind of impregnable sarcasm, nor with a surrender to a blind or exhausted acquiescence. Rather, as in the Japanese use of the term *sono-mama* ('just-so-ness'), it is a matter of 'taking things as they are' in a fundamental act of acceptance and celebration of life, which is in no way reducible to conservatism or resignation, let alone a sneering contempt or satiric defiance. Its kindred spirit, in fact, is none other than humour, which has its own salutary way of appropriating absurdity and irrationality. As James Sully has suggested, 'while satire, sarcasm and their kind seem to be trying to push things away, or at least to alter them, humour, curiously enough, looks as if it were tenderly holding to the world which entertains it.'[27] It is this tenderness that is evident in the *haiku*, or in Zen paintings such as Mu-ch'i's 'Monkeys' and 'Crane,' or in P'ang Chü-shih's carrying fuel and drawing water, or Yüan-wu's particle of dust and solitary blossom.

What, after all, is the 'point' or function or value to be assigned to the little wild flower – on the basis of which we might imagine ourselves capable of accepting and affirming and being grateful for its existence – the wild flower that, like the millions of generations that have preceded it, pushes its delicate face up to the sunlight filtering into the forest glade, and dares anyone to make sense out of it? Into what cosmic plan does one fit the millennia of dinosaurs, or the teeming life of the sea? Or what is the meaning of the butterfly that briefly climaxes a bizarre metamorphosis through several identities in a crazy zig-zag pattern of aimless flight? What is the sense in the meandering path of a mountain stream, or the sermon being given in the babbling nonsense of the brook? What is the purpose of the millions of galaxies and their billions of stars, or the use of the millions of common flies and their billions of eggs? And what of all the waste space in space – if not as a sign of the playfulness and sheer thereness (or not-thereness) of things which stubbornly refuse to conform to man's rational patterns and designs, or to his egotistic presumption that all things must defer to his moral and religious requirements?

> *The moor hens sing,*
> *And to their tempo – look! – the clouds*
> *Are hurrying.*

Issa[28]

Religion often deals with questions of meaning, purpose and value, and precariously attempts to assign a significance and structure to things. Yet at the same time it deals with that level of mystery, and absurdity, which transcends all such categories. And though it may expend considerable effort in defining and preserving, through symbol, myth and ritual, certain elemental truths and virtues which it feels itself compelled to uphold, still it falls far short of the *mysterium* out of which it arises, and to which it points, if it does not also affirm and celebrate the isness, the thereness, the sheer suchness of things, and participate joyfully in existence even when it doesn't play according to the rules and expectations set up for it. In Van der Leeuw's words: 'The religious significance of things . . . is that one which no wider or deeper meaning can follow. It is the meaning of the whole: it is the last word. But this meaning is never understood, this last word is never spoken; always they remain superior, the ultimate meaning being a secret which reveals itself repeatedly, only nevertheless to remain eternally concealed. It implies an advance to the farthest boundary, where only one sole fact is understood: that all comprehension is "beyond".'[29]

This appreciation of mystery, this delighted wonder, is not simply the consequence of some abstract reflection upon things, and therefore a rational dislocation that Zen is seeking to overcome. It is rather the profoundest level of human experience in relation to which man so often misguidedly entertains the rationalistic conceit of attempting to define and confine and, in the process, ultimately overcome this mystery. It stands as the limit, the boundary, the end of all thought. As Suzuki has expressed it, 'When a man faces this mystery one day in his life, he is filled with the mystic sense which goes utterly beyond intellection.'[30] Here it is no longer a matter of a problem to be solved, or a puzzle to be put together, or a curiosity that will open its peculiarities to patient observation. No amount of philosophical reasoning or scientific investigation or religious inquiry can net it and capture it and add it, like another species of intellectual triumph, to the informational zoo of human knowledge. The common confusion between this *ultimate* sense of mystery and mystery in the sense of *problem-solving* is remarkably absent in Zen, especially because of its sensitivity to mystery in the most commonplace, obvious, taken-for-granted – and therefore presumably well-known – areas of experience, and because of its radical critique of all rational attempts at definitively dealing with reality. Zen comes to terms with absurdity long before it becomes the traumatic problem, or reaches the crisis proportions, so familiar in Western philosophical and religious thought.

This fundamental experience of absurdity is not, however, a withdrawal into a sheer agnosticism which sees and knows nothing in relation to the mystery of the Void, and which in a sense of futility or despair, or in simple boredom or fatigue, turns away to more manageable concerns. Nor is it an absolutism in relation to which everything is now seen and known completely in some higher wisdom of omniscience. In Suzuki's phraseology again, 'All things come out of an unknown abyss of mystery, and through every one of them we can have a peep into the abyss.'[31] On the one hand this is an 'unknown abyss of mystery' with respect to which the claim to know the infinite depths of this abyss is only the comedy of a new ignorance and pretension. On the other hand, inasmuch as all things are manifestations of this abyss, and ultimately one with it, 'through every one of them we can have a peep into the abyss.'

It is this understanding that is captured in the utter simplicity and commonplaceness of Bashō's *haiku*:

> *Coming along the mountain path*
> *I am somehow mysteriously moved*
> *By these violets.*[32]

Such a perception, once more, can be interpreted soberly as the experience of awe and wonder, of marvel and amazement, of sublimity, when confronted by even so fragile and insignificant a particular as a violet turning its tiny face up to the light. But soberness is not enough, nor does it reflect the whole of the experience. With equal legitimacy this perception can be interpreted comically as the sudden awareness of the absurdity, the nonsense, the pointless thereness of the flower which, tiny and helpless though it might be, defies all attempts at coercing it into conformity with the categories of rationality and value and purpose, at fitting it into a system, at 'discovering' its utility, or at making it the object of desire, attachment and possession. The mode of perception and experience toward which Zen points is really defined by both moments and both expressions. It is the combination of sublimity and absurdity, of reverence and humour, of amazement and laughter, that arises out of the transparent thusness, yet ineffable mystery of all being. It is a level of spiritual and aesthetic achievement which, as Huizinga said of poetry, 'lies beyond seriousness, on that more primitive and original level where the child, the animal, the savage and the seer belong, in the region of dream, enchantment, ecstasy, laughter.'[33]

Notes

1. Sirén, **II**, 132.
2. Suzuki, **III**, 89.
3. Wu, page 250.
4. Suzuki, **III**, 77–8.
5. Grock, *Life's a Lark* (New York: Benjamin Blom, 1969), pages 17 and 52.
6. Wu, page 247.
7. Luk, **II**, 193.
8. *Pi-yen-lu*, case 95; Shaw, page 276.
9. Luk, **II**, 188.
10. Suzuki, **III**, 368–9.
11. Reps and Senzaki, page 68.
12. Chang Chen-chi, *The Practice of Zen* (New York: Harper, 1959), page 58.
13. Wu, page 266.
14. Luk, **II**, 187.
15. *Ibid.*, page 35.
16. Suzuki, **III**, 87, translates this: 'How wondrously supernatural, and how miraculous this! I draw water, and I carry fuel!'
17. Suzuki, *No-Mind*, page 104.
18. Blyth, *Oriental Humour*, page 91.
19. Suzuki, **I**, 257.
20. John Blofeld, translator, *The Zen Teaching of Huang Po* (New York: Grove, 1959), page 29.
21. Wu, page 40.
22. Blyth, *Oriental Humour*, page 89.
23. Suzuki, **III**, 59.
24. Henderson, pages 58, 151.
25. Suzuki, **II**, 249.
26. George Santayana, *Soliloquies in England and Later Soliloquies* (New York: Scribners, 1922), pages 141–2.
27. *An Essay on Laughter* (London: Longmans, 1902), page 384.
28. Henderson, page 153.
29. Gerardus van der Leeuw, *Religion in Essence and Manifestation*, translated by J. E. Turner (New York: Harper, 1963), **II**, page 680.

30. Suz uki, **III**, 319.
31. *Ibid.*, page 348.
32. S uzuki, *Japanese Culture*, page 262.
33. Joh an Huizinga, *Homo Ludens* (Boston: Beacon, 1950), page 119.

FIVE

Laughing at the Buddhas and
Abusing the Patriarchs

When you meet a Buddha, kill the Buddha;
  When you meet a Patriarch, kill the Patriarch.
LIN-CHI

The Nirvāna Sūtra?
  This is last in line for cremation.
CHĒN LUNG-HSIN

The abbot Kuei-shan (Isan) said of Tē-shan (Tokusan, 780–865)
who had visited his temple, walked back and forth in critical
examination, only to declare, 'There is nothing here,' and
walk away: 'That young man will after this go to some
isolated mountain top, establish a hermitage, laugh at the
Buddhas, and abuse the Patriarchs.'[1] And he did.

There has probably never been a religious movement more
sweepingly iconoclastic than Zen. Idols of every sort are
relentlessly and mercilessly smashed: not only the ego and its
desires and attachments, but scripture, doctrine, tradition,
meritorious works, liturgy, prayer, gods, miracles, Bodhisattvas, and even the Buddha himself. Much of the humour in
Zen is therefore iconoclastic in character; for before true
liberation can occur, all idols must be overturned, or stood
upside down. Anything, however holy, is potentially an idol;
therefore anything is a legitimate object of laughter. No aspect
of one's existence is to be elevated beyond the requirements of
humour, including one's existence itself. To take things too
seriously, let alone absolutely, however significant they might
otherwise seem, is to be dependent upon them and therefore
caught in the wheel (the vicious circle) of attachment, desire
and bondage. This is the chain of *karma* and the wheel of
samsāra.

Liang-k'ai's 'Sixth Patriarch Tearing Up A Sutra Scroll' is

indicative of the manner in which Zen handles potential idols, and by the same token sources of attachment, of every sort, including (and perhaps even especially) religious idols. Because anything that is categorised as holy may become simply a new, and more subtle, basis of dependence, instead of a vehicle for emancipation from the bondage of grasping and clinging, holy things must constantly be subjected to profanation. This capacity to profane the sacred, and to do so effectively, yet delightfully – and therefore all the more effectively – is, of course, the special talent of the clown and the fool. And the Zen appreciation for, and use of, the techniques of comic profanation is unparalleled in the history of religion and religious art. (See plate 7.)

Beginning with the first Ch'an Patriarch, Bodhidharma, the comic-iconoclastic motif is central to Zen, as in the tale of his audiences with the emperor Wu-ti of Liang. Wu-ti (465–550) was a very religiously concerned ruler who had expended large sums of money on Confucian temples and schools, and then, still unfulfilled in his spiritual aspirations, had turned to Buddhism. Again he spent lavishly for the erection of temples and for the immigration of thousands of Buddhist priests and monks to teach and disseminate the Buddhist way. For three periods he left his throne to become a monk, only to be coaxed back by his ministers of state – though his days ended during his last seclusion, in the Monastery of Harmonious Peace. In his conversation with Bodhidharma, Wu-ti is reputed to have inquired concerning his accumulation of merit: 'Ever since the beginning of my reign I have built so many temples, copied so many sacred books, and supported so many monks and nuns; what do you think my merit might be?' 'No merit whatever, sire!' was Bodhidharma's reply.[2]

Killing the Buddha

Nothing in the entirety of the Buddhist tradition is safe from the iconoclastic fires of Zen, not even the Buddha himself. The classic instance is that of master Tan-hsia's (Tanka, 738–824) burning of the Buddha-image. It was so cold at the temple where Tan-hsia was once lodging that he took one of the three images from the altar and burned it for firewood. (Plate 8.) When the horrified chief monk asked him what he thought he was about, and how he dared profane the sacred image of the Buddha, he replied that he was burning it to obtain its *sarira* (an indestructible substance believed to reside in the ashes of holy men). When the monk exclaimed, incredulously, 'How could a wooden Buddha have any *sarira*?' Tan-hsia replied, 'Well, there is no *sarira* so far; why don't we take the other two Buddhas from the altar and burn them too!'[3] Yin-to-lo's (14th century) painting of this episode shows Tan-hsia replying with a pronounced, and somewhat devilish, grin on his face as he warms his hands by the fire. A later depiction by Fūgai (1779–1847) brings out the comic-iconoclastic character of the incident in fullest absurdity: the two dominant figures in the sketch are the Buddha-image burning helplessly on the ground, and the pronounced backside of Tan-hsia as he gleefully bends over the flames.

In sharp contrast to all recognisable forms of piety and devotion, the Zen records commonly contain profanations of the name of the Buddha. A monk asked Yün-mén (Ummon), 'What is the Buddha?' His shocking reply: 'A wiping-stick of dry dung!' Similarly Tē-shan before him had declared, 'The Buddha is a dried piece of barbarian dung, and saint-hood is only an empty name.'[4] Chao-chou (Jyōshū) once declared, in typical fashion: 'The one word I dislike most to hear is "Buddha".'[5] And Lin-chi (Rinzai) offered this characteristic piece of advice to his monks: 'Do not take the Buddha for the Ultimate. As I look at him, he is still like the hole in the privy. As to the Bodhisattvas and Arhats, they are all cangues and chains to keep you in bondage . . . Do not deceive yourselves! I care nothing for your expertise in interpreting the sutras (scriptures) and shastras (commentaries), or for your high positions in the world, or for your flowing eloquence, or for your intelligence and wisdom. I only care for your true and authentic insight and perception. Followers of Tao! Even if you were able to expound a hundred sutras and shastras, you would still be no match for a simple and humble monk with no concern for anything.'[6]

Once when Lin-chi visited the stupa of Bodhidharma, the guardian monk asked him, 'Do you wish to pay your reverence first to the Buddha or first to the Patriarch?' Lin-chi curtly responded, 'I do not want to pay my reverence to either!'[7] It was Lin-chi's insistence that one must 'kill the Buddha' and 'destroy the Patriarchs' in order to achieve liberation and enlightenment; for even the Buddha and the Patriarchs can become a stumblingblock to spiritual realisation. 'Take this mountain monk's advice,' taught Lin-chi, 'and you can sit on and break the heads of the Sambhogakāya and Nirmānakāya Buddhas. Then you will regard as one of your servants a Bodhisattva of the tenth stage who has completely realised his whole mind; the two forms of supernatural enlightenment will be likened to a cangue worn round the neck of a prisoner; Arhatship and Pratyeka Buddhahood will be likened to ordure in the latrine; and enlightenment and Nirvāna to a donkey's tethering stake.'[8]

Similarly, when a monk asked master Fēng (Seppō) what were the essential teachings of the Buddha and the Patriarchs, he retorted: 'The Buddha is a bull-headed jail-keeper, and the Patriarchs are horse-faced old maids!'[9] The more recent master, Sengai, who produced a number of comic sketches, had the audacity to paint his own death scene with himself sitting in the hallowed place of the Buddha in the traditional *Parinirvāna* scene. It was also Sengai who was responsible for the incredible, by usual religious standards, sketch of a monk leaning over to relieve himself of intestinal gas, with the accompanying title, 'The One Hundred Days Teaching of the Dharma.'

This and many similar pieces of iconoclastic literature and art, comically profaning the whole gamut of Buddhism from the Buddha on down, take on additional significance when one recalls the more popular level of Mahāyānist piety that invaded China, as reflected in such a work as the *Butsu Myōkō* (Scripture of the Names of the Buddha). Translated into Chinese by the 7th century AD, it comprised twelve volumes providing the faithful with the names of no less than eleven thousand and ninety-three Buddhas and Bodhisattvas, the recital of which assuredly brought peace, prosperity, purgation of sins, merit and ultimately Bodhisattvahood.[10] Pure Land advocate Tao-ch'o (562–645) in his *An-lē-chi* (Book of Peace and Happiness) argues, in fact, 'Is it not said that even once thinking of Amitābha Buddha and uttering his name cleanses us from all our sins committed while transmigrating for eighty billion kalpas? If even one thought achieves this, how much more if one constantly thinks of the Buddha and repents one's [sinful deeds]!'[11] But when a monk asked master Ta-kuan (Takkan, 1543–1604) whether he ever performed the *Nembutsu* (repetition of the invocation to Amida Buddha, *Namu-Amida-Butsu*), he replied, 'No, I never do!' 'Why not?' 'Because I am afraid of polluting my mouth!'[12]

The tenor of much of Mahāyānist piety, in dialectical relation to which Zen stands as if almost completely divested of all religious sentiment, is expressed in a hymn of the 11th century:

> *Ah! Pity it is we cannot see the Buddha face to face,*
> *Though He is present always, everywhere.*
> *And yet, perchance, as in a vision, He will come to us*
> *In the calm morning hours, when no man stirs.*[13]

Relative to this much of Zen seems insensitive, impudent, and irreverent, if not blasphemous, as in the boldness of Ikkyu's (1394–1481) lines:

> *Śākyamuni,*
> *That mischievous creature,*
> *Having appeared in this world –*
> *How many, many people, alas,*
> *Have been misled by him!*[14]

Or in another of Ikkyu's poems he writes:

> *Why are people called Buddhas after they die?*
> *Because they don't grumble any more,*
> *Because they don't make a nuisance of themselves!*[15]

If Zen stands, as it does, within this larger Mahāyānist tradition, it does so most iconoclastically; and this iconoclasm is central to Zen from its earliest patriarchal period, contemporaneous with such texts as the *An-lē-chi* and the *Butsu Myōkō*, into the modern period.

Burning the Sutras and Shastras

With the Zen emphasis upon the 'wordless Dharma' it is no surprise to find that the Buddhist sutras and their commentaries receive their fair share of (symbolic and literal) tearing and burning. Han-shan carries a blank sutra scroll, Hui-nēng tears up a sutra scroll, and Tē-shan and Hsiang-yen burn all their sutras and shastras. The statement of Yün-mēn (Ummon) may be taken as representative of Zen iconoclasm with respect to scripture: 'What a mess are the Three Vehicles [the *Tripitaka*], the teaching of the twelve divisions of the Canon, and Bodhidharma's coming from the West! Is it not advisable to let it pass; and if it is not allowed to pass, is it worth a single shout?'[16]

The dangers of overdoing such an iconoclasm in relation to scripture are, of course, those of losing valuable points of reference, turning freedom into licence, and confusing ignorance with wisdom. And no doubt this occurred in varying degrees in the hands of lesser monks and lay disciples. As one contemporary critic of early Ch'an argued: 'The harm done from depending too much on the sutras and philosophical treatises is slight compared with the harm from positively ignoring them – an attack which is a great hindrance to properly following the Buddhist life.' The same author, a member of the rival T'ien-tai (Tendai) sect, cites the lament of another critic of Zen: 'The worst part of it is, indeed, that those ignorant villagers, after visiting the Zen monasteries and listening to sermons given by the masters, are inordinately delighted, and without giving much thought to the spirit of the teaching, declare themselves to be teachers, not only disparaging the ancient worthies but depreciating the sutras and their contents with their own incoherent utterances.'[17] Unfortunately this also describes something of the recent fate of Zen in the West.

No doubt Zen did play into the hands of an antinomianism and anti-intellectualism which simply failed to make the distinction between non-attachment and either cavalier disregard or blind ignorance. And the risks in such thorough-going iconoclasm are very real, and should not be minimised. Ridicule can easily become an end in itself, or a subtle technique of rationalisation, going nowhere, destroying, and putting nothing in its place. And it can easily be exploited as a justification for indolence, or for regression to childish forms of impulsive behaviour, obeying only the whims of the moment. On the other hand, any method is subject to misuse and misinterpretation, and one must assume that the Zen masters were as aware of the problem as their critics. Such seems to be intimated in the comment of Yang-shan (Kyozan, 750–834) that those coming to him received, and could only be given, what they were seeking: 'Shih-t'ou keeps a shop dealing in solid gold only, but mine handles a variety of wares. If a man comes for a rat's droppings, I let him have them. If he wants solid gold, I also meet his wish.'[18]

Tai-hui (Daiye, 1089–1163) makes clear the necessity of mediating between extremes in his letter to a disciple: 'There are two forms of error now prevailing among followers of Zen, laymen as well as monks. The one thinks that there are wonderful things hidden in words and phrases, and those who hold this view try to learn many words and phrases. The second goes to the other extreme forgetting that words are the pointing finger, showing one where to locate the moon ... They reject all verbal teachings and simply sit with eyes closed, letting down the eyebrows as if they were completely dead.'[19] Both are forms of attachment and bondage; therefore, both must be subjected to iconoclasm. I-tuan, a disciple of Nan-ch'uan (Nansen), expressed the matter more simply and epigrammatically to his assembly: 'Speech is blasphemy, silence a lie. Above speech and silence there is a way out.'[20]

The defence of Zen's 'tearing and burning' scripture is put

in a characteristic manner by Tai-chu (Daishi): 'Awakened to reality, they throw away the doctrine, just as a fisherman, having caught his fish, pays no more attention to his nets; or as a hunter, after catching his rabbit, forgets about his snare.'[21] Chuang-tzu much earlier (4th century BC) had written the same, adding:

> The purpose of words is to convey ideas;
>   When the ideas are grasped, the words are forgotten.
> Where can I find a man who has forgotten words?
> He is the man I would like to talk to.[22]

But this is all from the standpoint of having caught the game, or located the moon. Thus, the same Lin-chi that kills Buddhas and Patriarchs, and discards sutras and shastras in favour of a good shout, also insists that 'only a greatly enlightened person dares to slander the Buddha and Patriarchs, criticise people all over the country, repudiate the teaching of the *Tripitaka*, and insult and humiliate small lads and those who want to seek something in favourable or adverse circumstances.'[23]

Zen Parody of Zen

Given, however, the Zen attitude toward, and use of, scripture, this only added to the crucial importance of the masters themselves, their own spiritual realisations, their ability to communicate them, and to evoke, guide and test such in their disciples. All of this opened up another potential source of dependence and attachment, much like that of a Western patient in relation to his psychoanalyst. The 'wordless Dharma' also demanded a different sort of authentic transmission than that of scriptural texts. In order to verify the legitimacy of Zen as a Buddhist sect, and to establish its authenticity in relation to the challenges of rival sects, certain Zen enthusiasts as early as the 8th century had worked out a direct line of apostolic succession through 33 patriarchs, 28 of them Indian and 6 (counting Bodhidharma both ways) Chinese, to which was later added the legend of the Buddha's transmission of the silent teaching to the first patriarch, Kāśyapa. Though Zen might successfully, therefore, avoid attachment to scripture and creed, and dependence upon verbal teachings and rational arguments, its result might be only that of establishing a new form of attachment and dependence in relation to the Zen master himself. And while undoubtedly there were those who succumbed to this temptation, it is to the credit of Zen masters and disciples alike that the same comic iconoclasm which they turned toward all other forms of bondage was also commonly turned toward the master, the patriarchs, and the apostolic succession as well. This, in itself, to say the least, is an unusual phenomenon in the history of religions.

A classic instance of this is to be found in Shū-an's preface to Wu-mēn's (Mumon) *Gateless Barrier to Zen Experience*, whose 48 cases have served as a basic Zen text since the 13th century:

> If it be said that there is no gate by which to enter Zen, everyone on earth will enter by it; and if it be said that there is a gate, our master will find no ground on which to erect this (gateless barrier to Zen experience).
>
> He has commented thoroughly on the text from beginning to end, and this is like putting one hat on top of another.
>
> I am urged to praise this book (by writing a preface). This, again, is as foolish as crushing a dry bamboo to get juice.
>
> When one happens on a book of this kind, he is well advised to throw it away without waiting for the advice of an old man like myself, who would do just that . . .[24]

As if the point were not sufficiently underlined by the preface, and by Wu-mēn's commentary and verse on the text which is often as humorous and iconoclastic as the preface, an appendix of the same order is offered as a forty-ninth case by the scholar-statesman and Zen adept, Amban:

> The venerable Wu-mēn made the words of forty-eight cases, and judged the ancient worthies' *kōans*. He is like a fried-bean-cake seller. The buyers have their mouths

opened and the cakes pushed in until they are full, and they can neither swallow them nor disgorge them. That is what it is like. But Amban wants to add another extra cake . . . I don't know where the Roshi will put his teeth into it. If he can swallow it, he will emit light and move the earth. If he cannot, I will fry them all up together again.[25]

This inner-directed iconoclasm is also illustrated in the way in which so many collections of cases of *kōans*, *mondōs* and anecdotes from earlier masters are commonly handled by the later master who edits them, or re-edits them by freely re-interpreting them, perhaps rejecting the earlier interpretation or use of the materials, or the behaviour of the previous master on such and such an occasion. This approach, epito-mised in Wu-mēn's commentary and verse in the *Wu-mēn-kuan*, and the 'hat piled upon hat' of the preface and appendix, is referred to as *nenko* or *nenro*, meaning 'to pick up and play' with the master's materials, often humorously parodying his words and ridiculing his actions. Even the verbal and be-havioural heritage of the master is not sacrosanct. The con-trast with the warnings that often accompany sacred texts and utterances, such as that which concludes the Christian *Revela-tion of St. John*, is striking indeed:

I warn every one who hears the words of the prophecy of this book: if any one adds to them, God will add to him the plagues described in this book; and if any one takes away from the words of the book of this prophecy, God will take away his share in the tree of life and in the holy city, which are described in this book.[26]

Any attempt, likewise, at developing and defending a philosophical or doctrinal orthodoxy, even under the claim of representing a Zen philosophy and doctrine, is submitted to the iconoclastic fires of Zen. The Zen inclination is to constantly burn its own scriptures and commentaries. In one Zen tale visiting monks at Fa-yēn's temple were arguing over the philosophical questions of the relationship of mind to reality, attempting to apply the teachings of scriptures and masters to the problem. Fa-yēn (Hogen) interrupted with the question, 'Here is a large boulder. Do you say that it is inside or outside your mind?' One of the monks confidently hastened what he took to be the orthodox reply: 'From the Buddhist viewpoint everything is an objectification of mind, so that I would have to say that the stone is inside my mind.' 'Your head,' quipped Fa-yēn, 'must be very heavy.'[27]

On the other hand, even Zen as a meditational discipline and practice, however much it may suggest itself as essential to Zen as Zen (i.e., as the very meaning of the term, deriving from the Sanskrit, *dhyāna*, meditation), and as crucial to the 'wordless Dharma,' must not be permitted to absolutise itself as method or form. Otherwise Zen has only established a new orthodoxy, and therefore a new point of attachment and dependence. Thus, one of the earliest masters, Huai-jang (Êjō, 677–744) in conversation with Ma-tsu (Baso) asks: 'In learning sitting-in-meditation (*zazen*), do you aspire to learn the sitting Ch'an or to imitate the sitting Buddha? If the former, Ch'an does not consist in sitting or in lying down. If the latter, the Buddha has no fixed postures. The Dharma goes on forever, and never abides in anything. You must not therefore be attached to nor abandon any particular phase of it. To sit yourself into Buddha is to kill the Buddha. To be attached to the sitting posture is to fail to comprehend the essential principle.'[28]

Perhaps the most sacrosanct element in Zen, then, is the stress on the 'wordless Dharma,' faithfully transmitted from the Buddha through the patriarchs, and summarised in the so-called 'Zen creed' attributed to Nan-chū'an (Nansen):

> *A special transmission outside the scriptures;*
> *No dependence upon words and letters;*
> *Direct pointing at the soul [inner being] of man;*
> *Seeing into one's nature, and the attainment of Buddhahood.*[29]

Yet there are instances of both the transmission and the teaching being parodied, as in Wu-mēn's (Mumon) commentary on the legend:

A long time ago when the World Honoured One was dwelling on Vulture Peak, he picked up a flower and showed it to the congregation. They all remained unmoved, but the venerable Mahākāśyapa smiled. The Honoured One said: 'I have in my hand the doctrine of the right Dharma which is birthless and deathless, the true form of no-form and a great mystery. It is the message of non-dependence upon words and letters and is transmitted outside the scriptures. I now hand it to Mahākāśyapa.'

[Wu-mēn's commentary]: Golden-faced Gautama behaved outrageously. He reduced the sublime to the simple. He sold dog meat for mutton and thought it wonderful to do so. Had the whole congregation smiled, to whom would he have transmitted the right Dharma? Had Mahākāśyapa not smiled, to whom would he have transmitted it? If you say that the right Dharma can be transmitted, the golden-faced old man deceived the world. If it cannot be, how could he give the message to Mahākāśyapa?

> *When he held up a flower*
> *His secret was revealed.*
> *When Mahākāśyapa smiled*
> *No one in heaven or on earth knew what to make of it.*[30]

The fate of Bodhidharma, revered founding father of the Ch'an school and symbol of so much in Zen, is no different. Wu-mēn's commentary on the forty-first case of Zen 'teaching' is no less iconoclastic:

The broken-toothed barbarian [Bodhidharma] came hundreds of thousands of miles (!) across the sea proudly [to China], seeming to stir up waves on a windless day. Later he instructed a pupil and crippled him [Hui-k'o]. Alas, the fisherman does not know his ABC's.

> *A direct message from the West [India]*
> *Is in this story:*
> *The troublemaker for Zen monasteries*
> *Is you, the guilty one [Bodhidharma].*[31]

Perhaps it is not entirely inappropriate to Bodhidharma's character and the character of Zen that, based on the legend of his meditation for nine years facing the wall of a cave until his legs rotted out from under him, he later became the humorous Japanese 'daruma doll' whose pear-shaped figure has no legs, and, like the invincible clown, however toppled over, stands up again – as well as a snowman for Japanese children.[32] An old Japanese *senryu* adds the final *reductio ad absurdum*:

> *In another hundred years,*
> *Only Daruma's head would have been left.*[33]

Even the most sacred moments of Zen experience are not exempt from comic profanation and the humbling qualifications of humour, as in the episode of the enlightenment of Tung-shan Shou-ch'u (Tōzan Shusho). The story is one of four cases given by Tai-hui (Daiye) in a letter of advice to his disciple, Lü Chi-i. In the exuberance over his awakening, Tung-shan had exclaimed to his master, Yün-mēn (Ummon): 'After this I shall build my little hut where there is no human habitation; not a grain of rice will be kept in my pantry, not a stalk of vegetable will be growing on my farm. And yet I will abundantly treat all the visitors to my hermitage from all parts of the world; and I will even draw off all the nails and screws of their attachment. I will make them part with their greasy hats and ill-smelling clothes, so that they are thoroughly cleansed of dirt and become worthy monks.' Yün-mēn twitted him: 'What a large mouth you have for a body no larger than a cocoanut!'[34] Yün-mēn was quick to detect a potential reversion to egoistic pride, and the possibility of a new idolatry, in the zealous compassion of a fledgling Bodhisattva who was now self-assuredly about to enter the fanaticism of saving the whole world.

In Zen iconoclasm the relationship between the sacred and the comic is really the same as in all polarities that stand in dialectical relationship. It is a dialectic which both heightens

the tension and annuls it, bringing it into a higher and profounder unity on that plane of experience in which both
elements are transcended and brought to fulfilment. This is
captured so well in Anagarika Govinda's charming description
of the juxtaposition of sacred dancers and ritual clowns in
Tibetan Buddhist mystery plays. The primary participants in
the ceremony are the gorgeously costumed and fantastically
masked representatives of superhuman saints and celestial and
demoniacal beings. They are the very personification of the
sacred and sublime relative to the profane and the ordinary. But
as these 'awe-inspiring figures solemnly wheel around, the
almost unbearable tension and exaltation, which has gripped
the spectators, is suddenly relieved by the appearance of two
grotesquely grinning masks, whose bearers are aping the movements of the sacred dancers, and seem to mock the Buddhas
and even the terrifying Defenders of the Faith. They are weav-
ing in and out of the solemn circle, gaping into the faces of the
dancers, as if defying and ridiculing both the divine and the
demoniacal powers. These, however, seem to take no notice
and move on with unperturbed dignity. The effect is astonish-
ing: far from destroying the atmosphere of wonder and sacredness, the juxtaposition of the sublime and the ridiculous rather
seems to deepen the sense of reality, in which the highest and
the lowest have their place and condition each other, thus
giving perspective and proportion to our conception of the
world and of ourselves.'[35]

This, in much less dramatic and ritualised form, is the place
of iconoclasm in Zen. Veneration and profanation, reverence
and irreverence, profound respect and equally profound
parody, are united in such a way that the total effect is not dis-
cord but an alerting dissonance, not a chaotic cacophony but a
dynamic rhythmic harmony. 'By experiencing opposite poles
of reality simultaneously, we actually intensify them. They are
like the counterpoints in a musical composition ... Seriousness and a sense of humour do not exclude each other; on the
contrary, they constitute and indicate the fullness and com-
pleteness of human experience, and the capacity to see the

relativity of all things and all truths and especially of our own position.'[36]

Notes

1. *Pi-yen-lu*, case 4; Shaw, pages 34–5.
2. Suzuki, I, 188–9.
3. *Ibid.*, page 330.
4. Hu Shih, 'Ch'an (Zen) Buddhism in China,' *Philosophy East and West*, III (April, 1953), page 22.
5. Wu, page 138.
6. *Ibid.*, page 211.
7. *Ibid.*, pages 196–7.
8. Luk, II, 114.
9. Suzuki, III, 373.
10. Shaw, page 32, n. 4.
11. Suzuki, II, 146.
12. *Ibid.*, page 55 n. 3.
13. M. Anesaki, *Buddhist Art in Relation to Buddhist Ideals* (Boston: Houghton Mifflin, 1923), page 28.
14. Blyth, *Oriental Humour*, page 266.
15. Blyth, *Zen Classics*, V, 188.
16. Luk, II, 208.
17. Suzuki, III, 69.
18. *Ibid.*, page 58.
19. Suzuki, II, 85.
20. Wu, page 250.
21. John Blofeld, translator, *The Zen Teaching of Hui Hai* (London: Rider, 1962), page 123.
22. Merton, xxvi, 11.
23. Luk, II, 121.
24. Ogata, page 85.
25. Blyth, *Zen Classics*, IV, 321.
26. *Revelation* 22:18, 19 (RSV).
27. Reps and Senzaki, page 65.
28. Wu, page 92.
29. Suzuki, I, 176.
30. *Wu-mēn-kuan*, case 6; Ogata, pages 98–9.
31. *Ibid.*, case 41, page 125.
32. Joly, pages 120–2.
33. Blyth, *Oriental Humour*, page 414.
34. Suzuki, II, 27.
35. *The Way of the White Clouds* (London: Hutchinson, 1956), page 176.
36. *Ibid.*, pages 176–7.

SIX

The Folly of the Desiring Self

A monk once announced himself, giving his full name.
Master Tung-shan asked, 'Which one is your real self?'
The monk replied, 'The one who is standing before you.'
'What a pity!' responded Tung-shan. 'People of today
are all like this. They take the front of an ass,
or the rear of a horse, and call it themselves!'
TRANSMISSION OF THE LAMP

Zen folly is the other side of human folly: the comic reflection
of ego, ignorance, desire and attachment. Foolishness is sometimes best overcome, not by a grand display of wisdom and
spiritual counsel, but by a higher foolishness – which is one of
the reasons religions need not only masters and seers, but
clowns and fools, or masters and seers who (as they often are)
are both. The foolishness of the sage is the wisdom for fools;
and the impiety of the holy man is the means of salvation from
the false piety of the unenlightened. In his apparent madness is
revealed the real madness of the desiring self; his seeming
ignorance mocks the world of ignorance into which man falls;
and his nonsense proceeds from and invokes the beyond of
rational sense.

The comic folly of ego, ignorance and desire is effectively
captured in the tale of the monkey-man, Sun Wu-kung, in the
Chinese Buddhist *Travels in the West* (an account of the journey
of Hsuan-tsang to India, 629–45). Sun Wu-kung, as he is called
in the Chinese version, was proud of his exceptional somer-
saulting abilities, and saw his identity as defined (and threatened) in these terms. But the Buddha suggested that he could
not even jump out of his hand. Sun Wu-kung promptly pro-
ceeded to leap to the outermost reaches of the universe. There
he found five pillars, on one of which he wrote with a flourish
that he, the great monkey-man, had been there. And, after

thus extolling his feat and his virtue, he smugly and confidently returned to inform the Buddha of his accomplishment. The Buddha thereupon held out his hand, showing Sun Wu-kung the writing on one of his fingers. The joke was on Sun Wu-kung.

The Comedy of Ego, Ignorance and Desire

The fool and his folly is commonly the subject of comedy, particularly the fool who is blissfully unaware of his folly, and more particularly the fool who mistakes his folly for wisdom. This, in Zen, describes the self-portrait of man. Humour is therefore not only a permissible but especially appropriate way of getting at what in Buddhism generally has consistently been identified as the fundamental folly of the desiring self. If the ego is understood as one of the elements of the human problem, then humour corresponds to the realisation of the comedy of the substantial ego, the refusal to take the ego seriously or absolutely in its pretension of being the one secure point of reference in consciousness – as in the philosophy of Descartes where, when all else is in doubt, one retreats to the seemingly impregnable refuge of the reflective self: *cogito ergo sum*. There is no small irony in the fact that what is the fundamental illusion for Buddhist experience is taken as the fundamental axiom of Cartesian thought. In Zen, especially, it is through humour that the ego is revealed as only the mask that the actor puts on, or holds in front of his face (as in the *Noh* play, or ancient Greek drama, or the original meaning of the Latin *persona* as 'mask'), hiding his true identity, a mask which is both a tragic mask from the standpoint of ignorance and suffering, and a comic mask from the standpoint of enlightenment and liberation.

One is reminded in this of the bauble carried by many jesters and clowns in medieval and renaissance Christendom, with a carved representation serving as the head of the bauble-stick of themselves in their official identity and social role as fools. Common practice was to engage, in this fashion, in an extended conversation or debate with one's 'self.' The ego, as it were, was conveniently placed by the fool on the end of a stick for purposes of discussion, argument and disputation, or simply for hitting other people over the head![1] And that, in Zen terms, is the meaning of ego. It is the mask which the fool wears, or ties to the end of his stick, but which has a way of gaining an autonomy and objective reality of its own, so much so that the fool (as a fool) comes to identify himself with it, and even to enter into the prolonged debate of the divided self. This the clown and jester, as fools, have a special talent for exposing: the artificiality and insubstantiality of the ego-mask, and the schizophrenia which it engenders within the self, and between self and world.

This point is very simply made in the story of Keichu, a Zen master of the Meiji period. The Governor of Kyoto paid Keichu the honour of a visit. His presence was announced to the Zen master by an attendant who presented the Governor's calling card, which read: 'Kitagaki, Governor of Kyoto.' 'I have no business with such a fellow,' snapped Keichu to the attendant, refusing to see him. 'Tell him to get out of here!' When this was communicated to the Governor, instead of his becoming incensed, he took a pen and scratched out the words, 'Governor of Kyoto,' and gave the card back to the attendant. When Keichu saw the card, he exclaimed, 'Oh, is that Kitagaki! I wish to see him!'[2]

Through clownishness and humour, generally, the identities and distinctions to which we commonly give the utmost importance, and upon which we bestow the utmost seriousness and sacrality, are broken down. The rigidity and oppressiveness of the delineations of self and other, important and unimportant, good and bad, holy and unholy, great and small, are dissolved. And to the extent that this is so we are freed to laugh at ourselves and at the significance which we attach to ourselves, our roles, our boundaries, and our protective fences. The possibility is opened for us to hear, in Charles Morris' words,

> *The selfless laughter*
> *that can Buddha after Buddha*
> *spawn . . .*[3]

Here, as Suzuki says of his *satori*, 'my individuality, which I found rigidly held together and definitely kept separate from other individual existences, becomes loosened somehow from its tightening grip and melts away into something indescribable, something which is of quite a different order from what I am accustomed to.'[4] Similarly, Kōsen Imakita says of his awakening: 'There was no before and after. Everything was as though suspended. The object of my own meditation and my own self had disappeared. The only thing I felt was that my own innermost self was completely united and filled with everything above and below and all around.'[5] Yün-mēn (Ummon) put it quite differently: when asked by a monk what Niu-t'ou (594–657) was like after he had seen the Fourth Patriarch, and been enlightened, he replied, 'A cricket swallowing a tiger in a fire.'[6] That is, the small 'self' had been opened out to the infinite 'Self which is no-Self' through the burning up of ego and its pretensions and self-deceptions. In the new and larger perspective that such an awakening brings, one penetrates Wei Wu Wei's 'open secret' that '"self" and "other" are the oldest and most ubiquitous pair of clowns – the very archetypes of all clowns and of all clownishness.'[7]

Similarly, if one takes the Buddhist emphasis upon the problematic of desire, there is something not only pathetic but comic about passion, greed, envy, jealousy, pride and hatred. And one is fully liberated only when he sees both its pathetic and its comic side, both the suffering and the folly of his insatiable grasping and inordinate profession. Thus an aspect of the experience of enlightenment in Zen may be seen as the realisation of the forms of one's ignorance as foolish and therefore humorous, so that a part of what the liberation of an awakening may mean is the freedom to laugh at the comedy of one's blindness, and to laugh in the joy of new-found insight. After all, tragic folly is also comic folly and not simply and oppressively tragic. Ignorance is blind, yet also blissfully stupid and bungling. The figure of the man of ego and passion, like that of the dog chasing its tail, is simultaneously pitiful and funny. For this reason the clown and fool, as the laughable personifications of nonsense and folly, can serve, in their own buffoonish way, as agents of awakening and illumination. They are the crooked fingers pointing to the moon.

The image of the fool is a common one in Buddhist teaching, as exemplified in the frequency of the term in the *Dhammapada*. It is the unwitting self-portrait of man; and the clown-fool offers himself as the mirror in which man can see his reflection.

> *'These sons belong to me, and this wealth belongs to me,'*
>   *With such thoughts a fool is tormented.*
> *He himself does not belong to himself;*
>   *How much less sons and wealth?*
> *The fool who knows his foolishness is wise at least so far.*
>   *But a fool who thinks himself wise,*
>   *He is called a fool indeed . . .*
> *Fools of little understanding are their own greatest enemies,*
>   *For they do evil deeds which must bear bitter fruit.*[8]

Likewise in Zen a part of the folly of the self desiring to make conquest of the not-self is that the result is the opposite of the intention: the possessor becomes the possessed. The desire to achieve dominion over persons and things is involved in a comic/pathetic reversal in which persons and things gain dominion over the self. At best it becomes increasingly unclear whether 'the dog is wagging the tail or the tail is wagging the dog.' As in so much of comedy, in the moment of achievement everything is suddenly inverted, and the victor becomes the victim – though the humour in the inversion is only appreciated when the process is halted.

The teaching of Chuang-tzu is also that of Zen:

> *When he tries to extend his power over objects,*
>   *Those objects gain control over him.*
> *He who is controlled by objects*
>   *Loses possession of his inner self.*[9]

In Zen this applies equally to the intellectual attempt at grasping reality, at knowing in the sense of capturing and mastering things. Hence, a significant part of Zen iconoclasm is involved in the smashing of rational categories and value structures, the moral judgments and mental discriminations according to significance and utility which we interpose between ourselves and the world of our perception. For the true reality is hidden behind the boxes and badges of relative value, goodness and usefulness that serve instead to enmesh ourselves, as in a great net with which we have thought to trap reality, but have instead been trapped by our own devices. A monk once asked Ts'ao-shan (Sōzan, 9th century) the co-founder of the Ts'ao-tung (Sōtō) sect: 'What is the most prized thing in the world?' Ts'ao-shan responded: 'A dead cat!' The monk asked, 'Why is it so prized?' The master replied, 'Because no one thinks of its value.'[10]

There is something about this perspective, as in the comic perspective generally, that objects to the fixed, the definable, the formulated, whether it be legal, moral, social, or intellectual. And it does so not only because it senses this as stultifying the human spirit and stifling reality, but because it sees this as having an element of arbitrariness and illusion about it. In principle, therefore, it insists on the reality behind the façade, on the truth that resists final definition and formulation, or the outcome that baffles all canons of predictability. It defies all attempts at putting existence under the lock and key of rational law, moral convention, social structure, or considerations of worth or utility. Its adversaries are artificiality, consistency, and distinction, which it persistently thwarts with the surprises of arbitrariness, absurdity and inversions of value. In so doing it points to a state in which none of the categories through which the world is divided up and supposedly conquered exist; for categories are the weapons of discrimination and possession. And here, too, 'he that takes up the sword shall die by the sword.'

Comic Distance and the Bonds of Seriousness
Often this realisation of the folly of the desiring self is viewed only in terms of the dramatic mode to the exclusion of the comic. It is a 'serious matter' and not a 'laughing matter,' in

relation to which anything but the utmost gravity and solemnity seems inappropriate. Especially is this so inasmuch as
the realisation involved occurs in a religious context where,
presumably, one understands himself to be dealing with
issues of 'ultimate concern' that seem, if anything, to demand
the ultimate in seriousness. The comic side of this realisation,
and the importance of humour and laughter in relation to it,
therefore, is commonly brushed aside as peripherally, or just
accidentally, related to the difficulty and its resolution, if not a
part of the problem itself. The warnings of the German philosopher George Friedrich Meier are representative of the misgivings of more than German philosophers: 'We are never to
jest on or with things which, on account of their importance
and weight, claim our utmost seriousness. There are things . . .
so great and important in themselves, as never to be thought
of and mentioned but with much sedateness and solemnity.
Laughter on such occasions is criminal and indecent . . . For
instance, all jests on religion, philosophy, and the like important
subjects.'[11]

But from the standpoint of both Zen and the comic spirit,
seriousness itself, however noble its motivations and commendable its intentions, is also a sign of attachment and bondage. Seriousness is a part of the same entanglements which
seriousness would attempt to overcome. For implicit in all
seriousness is the inclination to take one's self and one's situation
too seriously. The fundamental problem, then, of ego, ignorance
and desire is, in a sense, precisely that of overcoming such
seriousness. Man 'falls,' as it were, when he begins to take himself and his separate identity, his desires and acquisitions, his
circumstances and fortunes, with the seriousness of one who
has made himself the centre of all things. In what he considers
to be an expression of his freedom, he loses his freedom by
placing himself in subservience to the demands of ego and
desire, and under the beck and call of anything and everything
that surrounds and affects him. Lin-chi's (Rinzai) characterisation of the result is most accurate: 'Look at the figure in the
puppet show, whose movements by another are controlled.'[12]

It is this that raises the issue of the peculiar relevance of the comic spirit and perspective. For the man with a keen sense of humour with respect to himself, his concerns and convictions, is to that extent a free man. He has achieved a comic distance which has refused that attachment to self and to things that spells bondage. He has not pinned his happiness and well-being to the conditions of his life or the consequences of his actions. And in the objectivity of a comic detachment he is not easily disturbed or threatened or conquered; for he has learned to laugh at the folly of the desiring self, its grand schemes, and its ensnaring involvements. This 'detached involvement' of humour which refuses to absolutise, and thus to endow with absolute seriousness, anyone or anything, is to this extent, at least, a corollary of the Zen emphasis upon non-attachment, and in its Zen form a part of what that non-attachment means. Hui-nēng (Enō) asks, 'What is Unconsciousness [*wu-nien*, or no-thoughtness, taking no thought]? It is to see all things as they are and not to become attached to anything; it is to be present in all places and yet not to become attached anywhere; it is to remain forever in the purity of self-nature; it is to let the six sense-robbers run out of the six sense-gates into the world of the six sense-objects, and yet not to become defiled therein, nor to get away therefrom; it is but to retain perfect freedom in going and coming.'[13]

On the one hand it is important to be serious, concerned, committed and involved; and these are praiseworthy virtues. On the other hand this in itself can become a new form of bondage, no matter how lofty its objective or how sincere its motivation. *One should not even be too serious about Zen!* The words of Ikkyu's *dōka* are the comic parenthesis within which the zealousness of all efforts at conquering the self and saving the world must be seen:

> *Though we do not preach the doctrine,*
> *Unasked the flowers bloom in spring;*
> *They fall and scatter,*
> *They turn to dust.*[14]

One of the things the comic spirit and perspective achieves is a capacity to be serious, yet not in such a way as to take oneself or one's aspirations *too* seriously; to be earnest, but not caught up within earnestness; to be actively involved, while not determined by this involvement nor attached to the outcome of one's action; to be sincere, but not imprisoned in one's sincerity; to live intensely, yet not tensely or in tension. Such an achievement makes possible a living in the world without being conformed to it or bound by it. As Yün-mēn (Ummon) phrased it, 'He speaks of fire without his mouth being burned by it.'[15]

As long as one is completely immersed in and therefore circumscribed, defined and determined by the little drama of the self and its situations, everything is quite sober and serious. A hushed mood of gravity and solemnity prevails; and trespassers on this holy ground must be punished or beaten off. The comic perception on the other hand is itself an emancipation, however momentary, from the fanaticisms of the ego and the tyranny of the situation. One has entered that freedom of spirit and liberty of detachment which opens up through seeing 'self' and 'situation' in a larger perspective. One has gone beyond seriousness and sobriety. As Suzuki comments in defence of the unusual comic emphasis in the poetry and art of the Japanese master, Sengai: 'An event becomes humorous when it is taken out of its limited frame and placed in a larger one.'[16] In humour there is transcendence and freedom. The free man is the one who is free to laugh, and to see things in the light of laughter. He is no longer in bondage to seriousness. What has been called the achievement of a 'cosmic consciousness' in the transcendence of the narrow, self-centred concerns and desires and attachments of an unenlightened consciousness, is therefore also a 'comic' consciousness. As Hermann Hesse writes in *Steppenwolf*: 'Seriousness is an accident of time. It consists in putting too high a value on time. In eternity there is no time. Eternity is a mere moment, just long enough for a joke.'[17]

One of the most important features of this achievement of

the freedom of a cosmic/comic consciousness is its impregnability. The serious individual, in the very act of endowing his person or cause or situation with an unqualified seriousness, has placed himself in the extremely vulnerable position of pinning his happiness and well-being to the precarious circumstances and fortunes of his existence. However grand the aspiration, however salutory the project, however commendable the ambition, the result is the same: one is intimately and inextricably tied to the result and its preservation. Seriousness, unmitigated, is a form of anxiety and craving, a restless clinging to self and grasping after the objects of its attachment. It is the posture and demeanour of one who is basically insecure and threatened, who has something to gain and therefore something to lose, who is afraid. The serious man lives essentially outside his 'self-nature,' in the objectifications of an ego-mask and the objects of its desire and possession. His equilibrium is placed in the hands of external factors and the whims of events. He is, therefore, to that extent, never free to laugh in the self-contained laughter of inwardness.

The distinct impression, on the other hand, of the realisation of the comic spirit and perspective in Zen is its invincibility – like the invincibility that has often been noticed in the person of the clown or fool. He cannot finally be conquered, defeated, or killed; for the Achilles' heel of ego, attachment and desire is not there. His life is not lived in the closed circle of seriousness. He seems to stand outside the common play of forces, like the clown or fool who stands outside the laws of society, of reason, and of anticipated appearance and behaviour. What for the ordinary man would be fatal – to his ego, his pride, his status, his image – the clown-fool accepts or ignores or shakes off with a resiliency that suggests access to some other plane of being. Like the comic characters in film cartoons who may be cut in shreds, smashed flat, riddled with holes, or stretched into a thin line, yet which suddenly spring back into their original form or are miraculously put back together, the clown always seems to survive. There is, as it were, no tree on which such a person can be hanged – as in the legend of the court-fool,

Marcolf, who so enraged King Solomon that he ordered his guards to lynch Marcolf, with the sole concession being that the victim might select the hanging-tree: 'So Marcolf and the servants travelled through the valley of Josaffat, and over the hill of Olivet, and from thence to Jericho, and over the river Jordan, and through all Arabia, and over the Grand Desert to the Red Sea, but they never found the tree on which Marcolf chose to be hanged!'[18]

The tragic hero dies, in a blaze of glory and a final shout of defiance perhaps; but the comic hero lives on. The clown-fool is therefore the unexpected, incredible, and yet very real symbol of freedom, wisdom, life, eternity. If the tragic hero, whose ego and pride and whose duty and world are intensely serious matters, belongs to death and winter, the clown-fool belongs, as Northrop Frye suggests, to spring and light and life.[19] In his own peculiar way he is the child of eternity and the agent of salvation. His innocence and ignorance, his non-sense and foolishness, his absurdity, draws upon some larger wisdom. The chaos which happens to him, or which he brings about, or which he is, is not death but new life, not darkness but light. It is the dissolution of the old order, the order of ego, desire and attachment, and the dawn of a new awakening and freedom. This is the other side of the double-image which he represents: not the archetype of folly and disorder, but the archetype of a new order and a higher being.

Beyond Striving and Seeking

It is in this necessity of going beyond seriousness that a Zen parody of Zen may be seen to be as important as an iconoclasm directed at the crassest forms of folly. When Ma-tsu (Baso) said that 'slippery is the road of Shih-t'ou (Sekitō),'[20] this was not meant as a criticism, but rather was a compliment to Shih-t'ou's skill in preventing any attachment to form, person, idea or scheme, any resting-place outside of the self-nature. Anything can become the object of desire, attachment and therefore bondage, including, as Hui-nēng (Enō) insisted, desire even for purity of Mind, or attachment to certain forms of meditation and spiritual exercise calculated to lead to this purity, either of which may only eventuate in another order of grasping and clinging. Hence his insistence upon sudden rather than gradual enlightenment; for true awakening and liberation must be that which flows forth naturally and spontaneously, and with an immediacy that precludes the distinction between what is sought for and the act of seeking for it. As long as one is in the process of seeking, one does not realise his possession of the Buddha-nature that is prevenient to his seeking, and the precondition of it. And if one already possesses the Buddha-nature, one does not really need to seek for it, as if it were elsewhere, or alien, but to acknowledge, use, and *be* it. Hence the act of seeking and striving must itself be turned into the non-act of not-seeking and not-striving. Action as such in this context involves the very sources of ignorance and bondage from which one seeks to be free: *ignorance* of the Buddha-nature within, *desire* for realising the Buddha-nature, *dependence* upon the means of realisation, and *attachment* to means and ends. As Chuang-tzu, long before the emergence of Zen in China, had written:

> *Joy does all things without concern;*
> *For emptiness, stillness, tranquillity, tastelessness,*
> *Silence, and non-action*
> *Are the root of all things.*[21]

In Japanese Zen there are, of course, important differences between the Rinzai and Sōtō methods of cultivating *wu-wei* (not seeking or striving). Rinzai Zen, in a sense, encourages seeking and striving through the use of the *kōan* method, in which one attempts to resolve the irresolvable *kōan* problem, and is required to offer a spontaneous answer to the master in periodic and often traumatic *sanzen* sessions. But, insofar as this encourages seeking and striving, it is in order to negate it by building up frustration and doubt to the point where all attempts to defend the ego and achieve a rational understanding and prepare an acceptable response are thwarted, and one is left with no alternative but to speak and act immediately and effortlessly out of one's 'original nature.' Thus, while from one standpoint the utmost seriousness and concerted effort may be required if one is to realise the freedom of enlightenment, from a larger standpoint such is not in itself the direct product of this seriousness and effort, in fact is not a product at all, but happens when one finally gives up, lets go, dies to self and desire, and exhausts all resources. It comes as out of nowhere, as if miraculously, as if by some special intervening act of grace. There must be a leap in the process, a break in the chain, analogous to, though not identical with, Kierkegaard's 'leap of faith' and 'suspension over twenty thousand fathoms.' In Hakuin's words, 'If you want to get at the unadulterated truth of egolessness, you must once and for all let go your hold and fall over the precipice.'[22] This leap into the abyss of emptiness in Zen is the 'snapping of the bonds of ignorance,' which is essentially an inward event, a manifestation of the self-nature, though commonly effected by some outward event, as in the case of Hsiang-yen's (Kyōgen) enlightenment on hearing the ping of the tile he had thrown striking a stalk of bamboo. The external event, however, stands in an accidental and absurd relationship to the internal releasing of consciousness, and the process that precedes it. Precisely what event it is becomes a miscellaneous datum. It functions as an occasion for the truth to manifest itself, but is not a part of that truth, in fact is finally irrelevant to it.

Sōtō Zen, on the other hand, in rejecting the *kōan* method and what appears to be the projected goal of having an *experience* of 'being enlightened,' argues that if one's original nature is 'Buddha,' then one is already within enlightenment, and there can therefore be no path *to* enlightenment at all. This would be like Po-chang's 'riding the ox in search of the ox.' The way of Zen is therefore *no* way, if by this one means a journey to some foreign destination. It is a way only in the sense of working out, or manifesting, or expressing, the fundamental character of one's being. Hence, as Dōgen (1200–53), the founder of Japanese Sōtō, insisted, one should 'just sit' for there is nowhere to go and nothing to achieve. There is no mountain to conquer, no spiritual ladder to climb, no river to cross. One is 'there' in one's self-nature from the beginning.

In this apparent conflict one recognises something of William James' classic distinction between the psychology of the *twice-born* and the *once-born*.[23] The Rinzai approach fosters the transformation of a consciousness that is seen as ensnared by illusions from which the individual must be released, and rescued from the false trails out of which the mind must be redirected. The Sōtō approach fosters a nurturing of a consciousness seen as fundamentally whole and pure, and needing only certain vehicles, like *zazen*, through which to develop and manifest itself. The Rinzai method, as Christmas Humphreys suggests, 'like the explosives used in logging, is designed to break the jam in the river, and let the waters and all which float thereon ride free.'[24] While the Sōtō attitude, in Alan Watts' imagery, is that 'muddy water is best cleared by leaving it alone.'[25] Originally, at least, these approaches must have addressed themselves to two different human conditions, though later they tended to become a matter of orthopraxy rather than a means of adjusting to individual differences.

Whichever the technique, however, both schools recognise that at a certain point (either from the beginning in 'just sitting' or through some dramatic change) the goal must become a non-goal, seeking must turn into non-seeking, action into non-action. As Bodhidharma is reputed to have said, 'All the attainments of the Buddhas are really non-attainments.'[26] Or as Hui-nēng (Enō) preached, 'When there is no abiding of thought anywhere on anything – this is being unbound. This not abiding anywhere is the root of our life.'[27] Similarly, the *Vajracchedikā* had defined non-attachment and non-striving as 'letting thought arise without fixing itself anywhere.'[28] In the moment of giving up the object of one's thought and desire and hoped-for possession is the moment of realisation.

On this point both Lin-chi (Rinzai) and Dōgen are in accord. Dōgen insists that the monk should be purposeless: 'Do not think about how to become a Buddha.'[29] Lin-chi, likewise, characterises the Zen man as one who has 'not a thought of running after Buddhahood. He is free from such pinings. Why is it so with him? Says an ancient sage, 'When the Buddha is sought after, he is the cause of transmigration.'[30] Therefore Lin-chi maintains that a true seeker does not seek. He 'simply walks when he wants to walk, and sits when he wants to sit, without a single thought of seeking Buddhahood ... Do not follow others who are busying themselves aimlessly with their studies of Ch'an and Tao, their learning of names and sayings, and their quest of Buddha, Patriarchs and enlightened masters ... If your searching minds really come to an end, there will be no more anxiety for anything.'[31] Hence the radical iconoclasm of Lin-chi's dictum that 'Bodhi (enlightenment) and Nirvāna are a stake to which donkeys are fastened.'[32] It is at this level that it is possible to say with Tai-chu (Daishu): 'No bondage from the first, and what is the use of seeking emancipation? Act as you will, go on as you feel – without a second thought. This is the incomparable way.'[33]

If the *kōan* method of the Rinzai school carries with it the danger of seeking to achieve the state of no-seeking, it must also be said that the *zazen*-only method of the Sōtō school involves the similar possibility of being trapped in the vicious circle of thinking about no-thinking, which thoughtlessness (*wu-hsin*) can only be achieved by a break, a discontinuity, in the ordinary processes of taking thought. Like the insomniac who attempts to fall asleep through the device of counting sheep, if sleep comes it comes not as a fulfilment of the process, but as its exhaustion. As Yün-mēn (Ummon) warned: 'Each of us carries a light within him, but when it is looked at it is turned into darkness.'[34] No amount of striving and purposing can achieve the state of no-striving and no-purposing, just as one cannot, in the strictest sense, give himself peace and tranquillity, which come instead when one has relinquished all effort that can only draw the strings of consciousness tighter. Though Zen aligns itself with the *jiriki* (self-power) approach rather than the *tariki* (other-power) approach, characteristic of the Jodo-shin emphasis upon faith and grace through the salvation of Amida Buddha, spiritual realisation is recognised as coming, not by self-effort as such, but ultimately by no-effort (*wu-wei*). This is not, however, seen as a boon bestowed from the otherness of some transcendent divine sphere, but as a self-manifestation of the Buddha-nature within.

The forty-first case of the *Wu-mēn-kuan* puts the matter bluntly, and in a style more characteristic of Zen:

> Bodhidharma sat facing the wall in meditation. The (future) Second Patriarch, who had been standing in the snow (waiting for an interview), cut off one of his arms (to demonstrate the sincerity of his seeking), and said: 'My mind is not at peace. Master, pray pacify my mind.' Bodhidharma replied, 'Bring me your mind and I will pacify it!' Hui-k'o lamented: 'I have searched for it, but cannot find it.' Bodhidharma said simply: 'There, I have pacified your mind.'[35]

Notes

1. William Willeford, *The Fool and His Scepter* (Evanston: Northwestern University Press, 1969), pages 33–9.
2. Reps and Senzaki, pages 31–2.
3. 'Utterance', *Festival* (New York: Braziller, 1966), page 82.
4. Suzuki, **II**, 33.
5. *Senkai-ichiran* (Tokyo, 1958), pages 71–2.
6. Luk, **II**, 199.
7. *Open Secret* (Hong Kong: Hong Kong University Press, 1965), page 167.
8. Irving Babbit, translator, *The Dhammapada* (New York: New Directions, 1965), v. 62–3, 66.
9. Merton, xxiii, 8.
10. Luk, **II**, 171–2.
11. *Thoughts on Jesting* (1764), edited by Joseph Jones (Austin: University of Texas Press, 1947), pages 55–6.
12. Luk, **II**, 95.
13. Suzuki, **III**, 36–7.
14. Blyth, *Zen Classics*, **V**, 175.
15. Luk, **II**, 185 n. 2.
16. 'Sengai: Zen and Art,' *Art News Annual*, **56** (November, 1957), page 196.
17. (New York: Holt, Rinehart and Winston, 1963), page 111.
18. Welsford, page 37.

19. *Anatomy of Criticism* (Princeton: Princeton University Press, 1957), pages 163–86.
20. Wu, page 140.
21. Merton, xii, 1.
22. Suzuki, **II**, 100.
23. *Varieties of Religious Experience* (New York: Longmans, Green, 1902), chapters 4–8.
24. *Buddhism* (London: Penguin Books, 1951), page 184.
25. *The Way of Zen* (New York: Pantheon, 1957), page 155.
26. Suzuki, **III**, 30.
27. *Ibid.*, page 35.
28. Max Muller, translator, *Anecdota Oxoniensia*, **I**, 1 (1881), page 27.
29. Dumoulin, page 164.
30. Suzuki, **III**, 54.
31. Luk, **II**, 114.
32. Suzuki, **III**, 54.
33. *Ibid.*, page 45.
34. Wu, page 215.
35. *Wu-mēn-kuan*, case 41; Ogata, page 125.

SEVEN Socrates in China

Nan-chu'an: 'Your body is unusually big;
isn't your straw hat too small?'

Huang-po: 'Though my hat may be small, the
entire universe is within it.'
TRANSMISSION OF THE LAMP

If the Zen master occasionally assimilates himself to the figure of the clown-fool, or introduces certain comic motifs and stratagems, this is not simply an end in itself, or even a personal actualisation of freedom alone, but also a means to an end. In full accord with the Mahāyānist emphasis upon the compassionate concern (*karunā*) of the Bodhisattva for the enlightenment of all, the truly enlightened one seeks, through a variety of techniques, including humour and clownishness, the awakening of the disciple. In a manner that is strikingly analogous to the Holy Fool tradition in the Greek and Russian Orthodox churches in which certain monks assumed the role of the fool, and engaged in odd or impious behaviour, in order to reveal the folly of the people, to awaken piety, and to conquer pride, the Zen master becomes something of a clown and behaves or instructs in unconventional ways in order to reveal the comedy in a false view of self, and to awaken a new perspective on existence. In a real sense, he is, in Enid Welsford's terms, the *punctum indifferens* and the fool as emancipator.

Precedent for this is already provided in the *Lankāvatāra Sūtra*, the favourite scripture of Bodhidharma, and therefore influential from the earliest period of Zen in China (6th century AD). The *Lankāvatāra Sūtra* refers to certain Buddha-lands in which 'Buddha-teaching is carried out by mere gazing, or by the contraction of the facial muscles, or by the

raising of the eyebrows, by frowning or smiling, by clearing
the throat, by the twinkling of an eye, by merely thinking, or
by a motion of some kind.'[1] This Buddha-land, thanks to a
Zen facility for bringing everything, including Buddhas and
Buddha-lands, down to earth, became in literal fact China and
Japan.

Hui-ts'ang (Ezō, 8th century), for example, asked one of his
monks, 'Can you get hold of Emptiness?' 'I'll try,' said the
monk; and he cupped his hands in the air. 'You haven't got
anything in there!' Hui-ts'ang exclaimed. 'Well, master,' said
the monk, 'please show me a better way.' Thereupon Hui-
ts'ang seized the monk's nose and gave it a hard yank. 'Ouch!'
yelled the monk, 'you hurt me!' 'That's the way to get hold
of Emptiness!' rejoined the master.[2]

Zen Midwifery

In this odd kind of relationship the master functions as a midwife of truth in the Socratic sense. And often this midwifery is
of a comic sort, or has a comic dimension to it – though it may
not be immediately apparent, as in the case of the painful
tweaking of the monk's nose. The master does not and cannot
teach the Truth in the sense of indoctrination; for the Truth to
be realised – an inward, intuitive, non-discursive truth –
cannot be dispensed in this way. It cannot, in fact, be dispensed in any way. This, of course, presupposes that the Truth
is present already, that one is already *in* the Truth, requiring
only the proper moments or occasions for its realisation. What
is demanded, then, is not a method through which the master
forces 'truths' into the mind of the disciple, but through
which, as it were, the Truth is beaten out of him. Tē-shan
(Tokusan), in fact, was noted for a most equitable use of the
stick on his disciples: whether they answered the master yes
or no, whether they answered in any way or remained silent,
they received thirty blows with the *keisaku*.[3]

The Truth, furthermore, is not only said to be within each
individual, which if left at that would seem to imply some
region that is to be explored and discovered, some place that

one is to commence in search of. It *is* one's innermost and uttermost reality. The Sixth Patriarch, Hui-nēng, whose teaching gave the definitive stamp to the subsequent history of Zen, expressed the point very dramatically: 'Our original nature is Buddha, and apart from this nature there is no other Buddha.' Indeed, 'all the Buddhas of the past, present and future ages, and the twelve parts of the Scriptures, are immanent in the nature of man as its original endowment.'[4]

Obviously, then, such a Truth cannot be given by one individual to another through some process of exchange, as one might pass coins from one purse to another. As Kuei-shan (Isan) said, in refusing to attempt to give any answer to Chi-hsien: 'Whatever I tell you will always be mine and will never concern you.'[5] One can at most be awakened to the Truth which is already within, and from which one has never been separated; for it is what one really is in himself. Such a Truth is necessarily inward and personal, not external and public. Chao-chou (Jyōshū) phrased the matter in terms of the 'low comedy' for which Zen masters have justly been noted. Once when asked by a monk what he saw as the most important principle of Zen, he abruptly excused himself, saying, 'I must now go to make water. Think, even such a trifling thing I have to do in person!'[6]

A critical term in Zen – and insofar as one can speak of a goal in Zen, the goal of Zen practice – is *kenshō*, 'seeing into one's nature.' As Tai-hui (Daiye) pointedly insisted in one of his sermons: 'The Truth is not what you hear from others or learn through the understanding. Now keep yourself away from what you have seen, heard, and thought, and see what you have within yourself.'[7] The Teacher therefore cannot 'teach' the Truth to the 'learner' as if he were a lecturer transferring previously unknown information from his lecture notes to the notebook of the disciple. And by the same token, the Learner cannot 'learn' the Truth; for it is a Truth which he already knows and possesses, in fact already *is*, but a Truth that must be *re*-cognised and *re*-alised. It is a Truth from which, in one sense, he has become estranged both in his knowing and being, and yet a Truth from which in the final sense he cannot be and never has been divorced.

There is consequently also no direct path to this Truth, as if the seeker were in one place and the Truth elsewhere, with the problem being that of locating the Truth and making one's way toward it like a pilgrim along some well-established route. As the 16th-century Indian guru, Kabir, put it (humorously):

> Path presupposes distance;
> If he be near, no path needest thou at all.
> Verily it maketh one smile
> To hear of a fish in water athirst.[8]

The 'Zen way' can thus be no way at all; for all ways are at best treadmills that permit the illusion of getting somewhere and learning something, and at worst endless detours which, if anything, get somewhere by proceeding further and further away. To avoid these ways is the 'way' of indirection. It is not a way which goes anywhere, or even proposes to do so, but which offers the possibility of opening one's eyes and seeing where one really is in one's inwardness. In the words of the four-character phrase, *chao ku hua t'ou*, commonly exhibited on the meditation halls of Ch'an monasteries: 'Turn inward the light on thy self-nature.'

The Truth that is to be communicated, then, cannot be communicated. It is not as if the master could hand everything over on a piece of paper which the monk could carry in his robe, or repeat in parrot-like fashion, or memorise and carry piously about along with the great variety of other bits of information, belief and opinion in the drawers of the mind. Yün-mēn (Ummon) warned: 'There are those who, upon seeing an old monk opening his mouth to speak, put his special words into their own mouths to chew them. They are like flies struggling to gobble up ordure.' Or again, 'If I speak words to teach you so that you can, upon hearing them, understand, I shall in fact be throwing ordure on your heads.'[9] Thus, when a monk, seeking informational knowledge concerning the famed Nāgārjuna – albeit a critical precursor of Zen, and the most important of the twenty-eight Indian Patriarchs claimed by the Zen sect – asked Yün-mēn, 'What is the school of Nāgārjuna?' Yün-mēn brusquely replied, 'In India there are ninety-six classes of heretics, and you belong to the lowest!'[10]

Though the *Lankāvatāra Sūtra* itself had defended the use of teachings and books for pointing and prodding in the right direction, at the same time it insisted on the constant dangers inherent in the substitution of propositional truths and abstract concepts for the Supreme Truth.

> Clinging to the external world, they cling to the study of books which are a means only, and do not know properly how to ascertain the truth of self-realisation, which is Truth unspoiled by the four propositions. Self-realisation is an exalted state of inner attainment which transcends all dualistic thinking and which is above the mind-system with its logic, reasoning, theorising, and illustrations.[11]

The real Truth is that Truth in relation to which all other truths are seen, that all-embracing perspective upon existence which determines all other perspectives, and which is existing-itself. It is a mode of perception and of being, where knowing cannot be separated from being, which affects the whole of one's being and knowing. It is therefore not a Truth of the same order as all other truths, and cannot be appropriated as other truths can. For one does not in this instance see and experience any specific thing differently; rather one sees and experiences everything differently. The conclusion drawn from this in all mystical contexts, however carefully adhered to in method and in fact, has been that such a Truth cannot, in the nature of the case, be transmitted at all, if by transmission is meant the delivery of something to someone who formerly did not have it and now is about to receive it. This would be to make the teacher into a religious peddler rather than a spiritual guide. If the term 'communication' is to be used at all, it can only refer to a process of provoking the 'learner' to an awareness of that which he already understands.

Socrates struggled with the same problem in the *Meno*. If such a Truth were not previously known, why would it occur to anyone to seek for it; and if one seeks for it, how could it be communicated to him; and even if communicated, how could it be recognised as the Truth; and even if recognised as the Truth, how could it be inwardly received and appropriated as the Truth? If, then, the Truth is to be knowable it appears that in some sense it must already be known, and that the issue is primarily one of finding appropriate techniques and providing appropriate occasions by means of which the Truth can manifest itself.

The Comic Occasion

It is significant that Socrates is noted, not only for his insistence upon inwardness and the maeutic relationship, but for his use of various comic ploys, and his adoption of the roles of iconoclast and fool. Aristotle refers to Socrates as the 'mock-modest' figure who in his understatement and feigned ignorance, and in both his refusal to teach anything and insistence on having nothing to teach, was a troublesome thorn in the side of the philosophical teachers and disputants of his day. Plato, also, though fearful of 'violent laughter' and critical of clowning and clown performances as such, has Thrasymachus in the *Republic* call attention to the element of buffoonery in Socrates' 'shamming ignorance' in an 'imbecile way' to effect a realisation of Truth. Socrates' role as 'gadfly of Athens' and impious iconoclast was, in fact, to a significant extent that of the clown-fool in his most profound and formidable form: one who has the disturbing capacity for bringing about the sudden remembrance of some understanding that lies buried beneath the sophistry of common discourse and doctrinaire pretension, even though he appears to be a simpleton who has nothing to offer, and from whom nothing is to be feared.

One is reminded in this of Ts'ao-shan's (Sōzan) advice to his monks: 'Keep your good deeds hidden and your function secret, that you may appear as a stupid and dull-witted man.'[12] Master Tai-chu (Daishu) used to say to those who came to him for instruction: 'I do not understand Zen, nor is there any special teaching to give out for your sake. Therefore, there is no need for you to be standing here for so long. It is best for you to get the matter settled within yourselves.'[13] Similarly, the Sixth Patriarch, Hui-nēng, when asked on what basis he succeeded the Fifth Patriarch, replied: 'Because I do not understand Buddhism!'[14]

The Zen method of instruction, then, is first and foremost, that of indirect communication. On the one hand this indirectness results from the realisation that words, even in their attempt to point toward reality, have a special genius for clouding and concealing it, and blocking the fullness and clarity of the very experience to which they would point. In Tai-hui's (Daiye) letter to Miao-tsung he writes: 'To talk about mind or nature is defiling; to talk about the unfathomable or the mysterious is defiling ... to direct one's attention to it, to think about it is defiling; to be writing about it thus on paper with a brush is especially defiling.'[15] On the other hand, because of the tendency of words to assume a kind of 'life' of their own, there is a great concern in Zen over the possibility that – comedy of comedies – the seeker of spiritual food will somehow mistake a knowledge of the ingredients and a recitation of the recipe for the meal itself, or that, worse coming to worse, the cookbook will be eaten instead of the dinner. Something of the old Taoist suspicion about words is also to be found in Zen; as the sage Chuang-tzu long before remarked: 'The men of old took all they really knew with them to the grave. [Their words are] only the dirt they left behind.'[16]

In Kierkegaardian terms, then, following Socrates, the master is not a teacher of truths, or one on whom the disciple is dependent for the truth, but merely an *occasion* for the Truth to manifest itself within the inner being of the disciple. This is the basis of his indirection. The master who offers himself on some other basis is a pretender and a deceiver. He sets up an external relationship to the truth, and places the disciple in a state of attachment and bondage to himself, when no such dependence can ever be forthcoming as a condition for realising the Truth. Though as Kierkegaard commented with characteristic wit: 'While no human being was ever truly an authority for another, or ever helped anyone by posing as such, or was ever able to take his client with him in truth, there is another sort of success that may by such methods be won; for it has never yet been known to fail that one fool, when he goes astray, takes several others with him.'[17] Socrates' conclusions from this are also those of Zen: the true master is a midwife. The midwife does not bring the baby, nor pass the baby from the stork to the mother, but assists the mother in delivering her own baby. Both the Truth and the condition for realising it are present already, requiring only an occasion, or 'intervening cause,' for its awakening.

The type of occasion afforded by the Zen master, however, is frequently identified by the peculiarity of being a comic occasion. And the comic occasion is, in fact, particularly suited to just such an indirection. A glance at some of the common features of comic lines, behaviour or situations reveals the close analogy between comic techniques and Zen techniques, as well as the serviceability of comic techniques in Zen: irrationality, contradiction, incongruity, absurdity, irrelevancy, triviality, nonsense, distortion, abruptness, shock, sudden twist, reversal or overturning. In both comedy and Zen one is prevented from drawing a purely intellectual conclusion at the end of an argument, and therefore entering the abstractness and deceptiveness of a pseudo-appropriation of the truth. The possibility of such an external relationship to the truth is short-circuited. This is delightfully illustrated in the tale of the first Ch'an master to visit Tibet. As was the custom, he was invited to participate in the traditional Tibetan debate which tests and displays, not simply the dialectical skill, but the spiritual realisation, of the monk. When the Tibetan monk, chosen to debate with the Ch'an master, had forcefully completed his opening challenge, the Ch'an master slowly rose before the hushed assembly and, after making the appropriate bows, without a word disrobed. Having thus revealed the 'naked truth' he sat down. The debate was ended![18]

The comic line or gesture actually goes nowhere, and in a literal sense, teaches nothing. Instead it calls everything to an abrupt halt. In a joke, for instance, the story seems to be getting somewhere for a time; the tale unfolds smoothly and rationally; information follows information in plausible order; and then, suddenly, the humorous twist throws everything into confusion. Instead of the story arriving at some reasonable conclusion or climax, the whole intellectual progression collapses. Yet it is just such a collapse that is the necessary antecedent to the realisation of another order of truth – whether in comedy or in Zen.

Many tales have arisen in the Zen tradition illustrating the use of such maeutic devices. A monk asked Ts'ao-shan (Tōzan), 'Are not monks persons of great compassion?' The master indicated approval. 'Suppose the six bandits come at them. What should they do?' 'Also be compassionate,' the master replied. The monk pressed further: 'How is one to be compassionate?' The master said, 'Wipe them out with one sweep of the sword!' 'What then?' asked the monk. 'Then they will be harmonised.'[19] Through this word-play the monk is supposed to come to the realisation, through the incongruity of a literal interpretation, that the six bandits are the sensuous desires which must be both 'wiped out' and at the same time harmonised. More importantly, he must come to the realisation that the moral of the *mondō* is really no moral, that the master's enigmatic reply is a refusal to moralise in the abstract. The humorous evasion of the problem as posed is a rejection of the terms of the question; for what is needed is not some prefabricated set of rules and recommendations for behaviour, which can easily lead to the illusion that to perform acts defined as compassionate is identical with being compassionate. The master comically distorts and confounds the issue as stated, for clearly the problem is not to arrive at a rational description of compassionate acts, but to become compassionate.

Chih-chang (Chijō, 8th century) one day announced a lecture

on the exemplary virtues of the Bodhisattva/goddess Kuan-yin (Kwannon). After his monks had assembled he said, 'When you have listened to the deeds of Kuan-yin you are able to behave properly in accordance with circumstances.' The monks, on hearing no further elaboration, asked, 'What are the deeds of Kuan-yin?' The master simply snapped his fingers; 'Do you all hear that?' The monks indicated that they had. 'This nonsensical company of yours; what do you want to get by coming here?' So saying, Chih-chang drove them from the hall with his stick, and laughing heartily, returned to his quarters.[20]

One of the most unusual features of Zen teaching is its ingenious and almost constant use of 'plays' upon words, ideas and situations – though to deal with them in any detail would require cumbersome notations on the nuances and idioms of the Chinese and Japanese languages and cultures. Suffice it to note the profusion itself of puns, idiomatic turns upon words, paradoxes and enigmatic sayings, startling gestures and acts. All have the same general intent of calling an abrupt halt to an unenlightened plane of perception, and projecting the hearer onto a more fundamental plane of experience. The disciple is never allowed to rest in an intellectual understanding or an attachment to names and forms. All such effort is kept in constant turmoil. Anything that does not point to or proceed from the 'self-nature' and one's 'original mind' is foiled and frustrated. All violation of ordinary meaning and rationality is of the same order and intent as the many other forms of Zen violence: the *keisaku*, the slap, the kick, the shout and the loud roar of laughter. The problem, as Fa-yen (Hōgen) put it, is that 'reality is right before you [and within you]; yet you are apt to translate it into a world of names and forms. How are you going to re-translate it into its original?'[21]

Kōan Nonsense and Mondō Playfulness

Behind this peculiar dialogic method of Zen lies the game of debate itself, with its premium upon cleverness, competitiveness and wit, and the demonstration of mastery through verbally defeating one's opponent, as in the confirmation of maturity and wisdom in Tibetan Buddhism through dialectical skill, or as in the Chinese Buddhist custom that a travelling monk may stay at a monastery if he bests a resident monk with the last word in debate. Much of this emphasis upon dialectical agility is to be found in Zen, as in the numerous tales of the meeting of two Zen masters, testing one another's enlightenment in what appears to be a 'can you top this?' series of riddles, double-entendres, non-sequiturs and ejaculations. In some accounts, in fact, the dialogue is purely playful, as in the contest proposed by Chao-chou (Jyōshū) one leisurely summer day to his attending disciple, Wen-yuan, to see which could 'identify himself with the lowest thing in the scale of human values.' The winner was to pay the loser a cake. Chao-chou began: 'I am an ass.' Wen-yuan: 'I am the ass's buttocks.' Chao-chou, 'I am the ass's faeces.' Wen-yuan: 'I am a worm in the faeces.' Chao-chou, unable to think of a rejoinder, asked: 'What are you doing there?' Replied Wen-yuan, 'I am spending my summer vacation!' Chao-chou conceded defeat.[22]

This in itself should not be taken as detracting from the method, for one must be careful not to make the role of games and humorous repartee only a serious one. Is it not permissible that even Zen masters should laugh and play? Otherwise we are only confronted with a new form of bondage to seriousness and a new reduction to utilitarianism, neither of which reflect the joyful freedom of enlightenment. The dialectical method as a method is, in fact, the invitation to this higher freedom beyond technique and utility, beyond seriousness and purpose, beyond means and ends. Rather than laughter and play representing the lowest level of attainment, they represent the highest; and the method moves toward rather than away from the spirit which they symbolise.

Even as method, there is a distinct element of play and of game in the dialogues (*mondō*) between master and disciple, many of which move back and forth at length, like the thrusts in a fencing match, with each manoeuvre by the disciple being deftly countered in an effort to bring him to the point at which his resources are exhausted and he is opened (cut open!) to deeper insight. Whether this is the play and game of humour or not – though one suspects that behind the awesome visage of the master there is a faint twinkle in the eye of one who participates in a higher knowledge, and thus who will very likely laugh loudly when the final blow is administered – the purpose of the wit and repartee is not to develop the dialectical abilities of the disciple. Nor is it to display those of the master. Rather it is to reveal the rational approach, and the dialectical approach as well, as a false trail. The master plays with the disciple, like a cat with a mouse, not however to destroy him but to awaken him, and to bring him to that level where he responds, not mechanically or even cleverly, but spontaneously out of his self-nature. Rather than the *mondō* being an exercise in sophistry, leading nowhere, it is really an exercise in what might fittingly be called a 'comedy of errors.' Once the error is revealed the disciple realises how awkward and artificial his clumsy responses have been, or how funny the question he has raised – as in the case of the monk who asked Ch'ang-ch'ing (Chōkei), 'What is meant by the True Eye of the Law?' only to receive the reply, 'I have a favour to ask of you: don't throw dirt around!'[23]

Similarly, in the last case of the *Wu-mēn-kuan* (*Mumonkan*) the tale is related of the monk who asked master Ch'ien-fēng (Kempō, 9th century), 'There is only one road to Nirvāna, and yet there are ten quarters of Buddha-land. Where is the true path?' Ch'ien-fēng raised his walking stick to draw a horizontal line in the air: 'Here.' On another occasion the same question was asked of master Yün-mēn (Ummon), who held up his fan and replied: 'This fan jumps up to the thirty-third heaven and hits the presiding deity on the nose, then comes down to the Eastern Sea and hits the holy carp. The carp becomes a dragon, which brings a flood of rain.'[24] Both answers are, of course, 'correct'!

In the same vein many of the paradoxical and seemingly nonsensical *kōans*, given to the disciple to meditate upon as a way of gaining release from an unenlightened way of perceiving the self and the world, have a comic dimension to them. This is not accidental, for the very provenance of comedy is nonsense and absurdity. Comedy plays with absurdity and revels in irrationality, turning it to its own ends. E. R. Hughes, in his analysis of epistemological methods in Chinese philosophy, notes that 'of all paradoxical writing in Chinese literature – and there is a good deal – the most paradoxical is that of the Ch'an Buddhist; and . . . I mean consciously and deliberately paradoxical, even with the intention of causing laughter, to make evident the incongruities in the human situation.'[25]

In this Zen employment of contradiction and nonsense is to be found considerable psychological insight. One may approach a false view of things by rationally pointing out its errors and cul-de-sacs in the grand manner of the philosopher; but often a more effective method is to do so absurdly and humorously. For once the ridiculousness of the viewpoint is revealed and appropriated comically, instead of having been driven into a corner and held at bay by the overpowering logic of the master, as in the *reductio ad absurdum* methodology pursued in the Mādhyamika system of Nāgārjuna – a position that may only be one of intellectual bondage in which the rope has been pulled tighter around the neck of the disciple – one has been freed to laugh, and therefore truly liberated. On the other hand, there is the distinct possibility in the discursive approach that the disciple will be tempted by the very intellectualism of the approach to seek some new way of overcoming the philosophical dilemma, some nuance that has been omitted or some angle that has been overlooked by the master – a tantalising defeat which may only perpetuate the argument, and hence the deception, *ad infinitum*. Something of the spirit and wisdom of the Zen method is captured in the account of Yang-ch'i (Yōgi, 992–1049) who rose ostensibly to lecture to his monks on the path of enlightenment, but instead began laughing and exclaimed simply, 'Ha! ha! ha! What's all this! Go to the back of the hall and have some tea!'[26]

It is because of this comic/socratic character of the Zen technique that one finds such a constant stress in the *kōan* and *mondō* upon contradiction, nonsense and absurdity – or at least apparent contradiction, nonsense and absurdity. As in Yün-mēn's (Ummon) answer to the searching question of the monk, 'When all mental activity is at an end, what is it like?' – 'Bring the Buddha-hall here, and we'll weigh it together!'[27] – it is as if one were suddenly plunged into the world of Lear's nonsense rhymes or of Alice in Wonderland. It is not, however, sheer nonsense. A truth is being pointed to obliquely and comically, for to point to it directly and philosophically would be both impossible and misleading. Nonsense does not mean totally without sense, but without sense in the customary view of the sensical, and beyond rationality in the ordinary understanding of reason. In nonsense one refuses to take with absolute seriousness – i.e., with humourlessness – the world of sense, whether of common sense or sophisticated reason. Nonsense is the question mark placed after the supposedly firm reality of the 'real' world of intelligibility, the irrefutable logic of rationality, or the categories and dichotomies of any system. It is this maeutic play upon irrationality in order to move beyond rationality that is expressed in Hakuin's familiar *kōan*, 'What is the sound of one hand clapping?' or in Yün-mēn's reply to the question, 'What is a sermon that surpasses the teaching of the Buddha and the Patriarchs?' 'Cake!'[28]

Many of the cryptic sayings of the masters do, of course, carry a great deal of symbolic freight. But even here, though they may be said to be filled with meaning, their enigmatic form is designed to mystify and thwart and therefore cut short ordinary processes of discrimination and appropriation. When the meaning becomes clear, it is not meaning in the sense of common rationality, and it refuses to be 'grasped' in such terms. A great deal of Buddhist teaching is here tightly compressed in the small chambers of the riddle or pun or 'gibberish' in readiness, as it were, for the explosion and burst of insight that must occur (or which in this manner is to be tested).

Very early in its development Zen distinguished itself from other Buddhist sects in China through the substitution of the much more 'socratic' *mondō* and *kōan* method of teaching for the sutra method, introduced from India, of recitation and exposition of scriptures and aphorisms. The sutra method easily lent itself to memorisation, interpretation and intellectual appropriation, but not necessarily enlightenment; whereas the dialogic and dialectical method of Zen constantly demanded interiorisation. Superficial, and essentially external, processes of assimilation were systematically frustrated. The Truth had to be appropriated inwardly and discovered in inwardness, or it could not be appropriated at all. It is thus that the scholar Tê-shan (Tokusan) came, with his knapsack full of Ch'ing-lung's commentaries on the *Vajracchedikā*, to a Ch'an mountain retreat to engage the monks in debate, intending to dispute and discredit Zen, only to remain as a disciple, and to consign his books to the flames. According to the Zen records he said in explanation of his act: 'An exhaustive discussion of the abstruse is like a hair thrown into the infinite void; and the fullest exertion of all capabilities is like a little drop of water falling into an unfathomable gulf.'[29]

It is difficult to imagine the word-oriented Near Eastern religions, with their stress upon the Word of creation, the prophetic Word, the biblical Word, the Incarnate Word, the kerygmatic Word, etc., including in their lists of holy men one who demonstrated his spiritual realisation by burning the scriptures, whether Torah, Gospels or Qurān – although there have been numerous instances of burning other peoples' books and bibles. But in a very real sense in Zen, as in mysticism generally, inner illumination implies the burning of all words. The Word of scripture or of reason is at most only an occasion for the realisation of that 'wordless Dharma' which is beyond all words, and in relation to which even the most sacred words stand in the awkwardness of hiding and obstructing that which they would reveal. The final word is silence, pregnant with meaning.

The comic/socratic character of Zen pedagogy is also apparent in the unusual prominence and extensive employment of a large body of anecdotal literature (which includes the *kōan* and *mondō* materials) – anecdotes which have a distinctively mundane, commonplace and humorous cast, and which function as a kind of Zen 'scripture' and meditation 'manual.' Anecdotal materials, to be sure, may be found in any tradition. But in Zen the role of the anecdote is much more central to the 'communication' of the teaching, and much closer to the 'point' of the teaching. The Zen tradition is not disseminated through a heavily symbolic ritual, or creed and confession, or scriptural canon, or catechetical indoctrination, or theological and philosophical disputation – all so familiar to Western religion. In the West the anecdote stands far more toward the periphery of the tradition, as a matter of popular discourse, sermonic illustration, ante-room banter, and the like. It is not at the heart of the teaching, either in terms of method or content, but is a kind of concession to those unable to ascend the lofty heights of theological, philosophical and ethical discourse, or unable to sustain such a level indefinitely without reprieve. In Zen, however, the reverse is closer to its peculiar genius. Without a focus in scripture, liturgy, myth, doctrine or metaphysics, the anecdote is more an official organ than an appendage. Rather than being a vehicle for popularisation, it points instead to that level of understanding and awareness that lies beyond all symbol, gesture and word, all reason and belief, even the most sophisticated.

The four largest collections of anecdotal materials indicate something of the extensiveness and importance of this remarkable 'scripture': *The Transmission of the Lamp* (1004–7) in 14 folios; *Five Lamps Meeting at the Source* (960–1279) in 20 folios; *A Finger Pointing at the Moon* (1602) in 10 folios; and *The Imperial Collection of Ch'an Sayings* in 14 folios. The very uniqueness of this anecdotal literature is in itself symbolic of the spirit and character of Zen. And given this kind of prominence, it is not surprising that, if for this reason alone, humour is also prominent in Zen. For though anecdotes are not necessarily humorous, they often are so. And in the very humanness, the everyday-ness of the tales of Zen masters and their disciples, the anecdote is much more likely to involve an appreciation of the comic than any other mode of religious discourse.

It might, of course, be a temptation to suppose that, because of the relative simplicity and ordinariness and good humour of the Zen stories, one has understood Zen in understanding the stories. The fact that they are quite commonplace and mundane, unlike the more esoteric character of mythological symbolism or the abstruseness of metaphysical speculation, would seem to lend itself to the false assumption that knowing Zen anecdotes is somehow synonymous with understanding Zen and experiencing an awakening. The peculiarity of Zen anecdotes in general, however, is the same peculiarity as that of the *kōan* and *mondō* in particular. Unlike the anecdotes to be found in most other religious traditions, there is usually no simple moral or lesson to be drawn from them which could conveniently be tucked away in the folds of an intellectual understanding, except the conclusion that there is no moral or lesson forthcoming. If the expectation is otherwise, one listens to the anecdote either with the pretence of understanding or with the same consternation, the same intellectual despair, the same sense of being logically short-circuited, the same feeling of being cheated or left hanging in mid-air, as in being confronted with a *kōan* as such. It is as if the entire anecdotal tradition were a big joke played on all anticipations of an easy mental comprehension and superficial appropriation. One sits down to what appears to be a plate of succulent and readily digestible fish, and receives instead a stone.

Even Shakespeare's fool, Bottom, understood the problem.

I have had a most rare vision. I have had a dream, past the wit of man to say what dream it was. Man is but an ass if he go about to expound this dream. Methought I was – there is no man can tell what. Methought I was, and methought I had; but man is but a patch'd fool if he will offer to say what methought I had. The eye of man hath not heard, the ear of man hath not seen, man's hand is not able to taste, his tongue to conceive, nor his heart to report,

what my dream was. I will get Peter Quince to write a
ballad of this dream. It shall be call'd 'Bottom's Dream,'
because it hath no bottom ...

A Midsummer Night's Dream IV. 1.

Notes

1. D. T. Suzuki, *Studies in the Lankāvatāra Sūtra* (London: Routledge, 1930), page 107.
2. N. a., *Zen Buddhism*, page 17. Cf. Luk, I, 136–7.
3. Suzuki, II, 48.
4. Wu, page 84.
5. Luk, I, 129.
6. Wu, page 146.
7. *Tai-hui-pu-shuo*, compiled by T'su-ching (1190).
8. Cited in Paramahansa Yogananda, *Autobiography of a Yogi* (Rider, 1969), page 349 n.
9. Luk, II, 189–90.
10. *Ibid.*, page 205.
11. Dwight Goddard, translator, *Self-Realization of Noble Wisdom* (Thetford, Vt.: Private printing, 1932), page 78.
12. Wu, page 188.
13. Suzuki, III, 43.
14. Wu, page 16.
15. Suzuki, II, 33.
16. Merton, xii, 10.
17. Søren Kierkegaard, *Philosophical Fragments*, translated by David F. Swenson (Princeton: Princeton University Press, 1936), page 7.
18. This tale was related to me by Lama Anagarika Govinda.
19. Wm. Theodore de Bary, *et al.*, *Sources of the Chinese Tradition* (New York: Columbia University Press, 1960), page 404.
20. Suzuki, *No-Mind*, page 92.
21. Wu, page 233.
22. *Ibid.*, page 137.
23. Blyth, *Zen Classics*, II, 58.
24. Senzaki and McCandless, page 129.
25. E. R. Hughes, 'Epistemological Methods in Chinese Philosophy,' *The Chinese Mind*, edited by Charles A. Moore (Honolulu: East-West Center Press, 1967), page 78.
26. Blyth, *Oriental Humour*, page 90.
27. Blyth, *Zen Classics*, II, 122.
28. Luk, II, 194.
29. Wu, page 152.

EIGHT   *Getting the Point of the Joke*

*When the approach to enlightenment is like
the swift thrust of a sword to the centre of all
things, then both worldliness and saintliness are
completely eliminated, and true reality is revealed.*
KUEI-SHAN

In the emphasis upon 'sudden awakening' particularly as
found in the Southern Ch'an school of Hui-nēng (Enō) and
its later Lin-chi (Rinzai) branch, is to be seen a further point
of correspondence between humour and Zen. Common to
both is the element of abruptness, in the one case an abruptness
which precipitates laughter, in the other case an abruptness
which precipitates awakening. And as has already been intimated, what the Zen masters have often done is to use the one
form of abruptness as an occasion for the other.

This relationship is by no means purely accidental, since the
sudden realisation of the point of a joke is directly analogous to
the sudden realisation of enlightenment, as this is interpreted
by Hui-nēng and Lin-chi. The point of the joke, or the humorousness in the antics of the clown, is something that is caught
immediately and effortlessly, or it is not caught at all. It does,
of course, require preparation in terms of setting, context and
mood – and here, as it were, the 'sudden realisation' school of
Zen includes rather than excludes the 'progressive realisation'
school. Nothing is more awkward and flat than an inappropriate joke, or a joke out of the context that permitted it to be
funny, or a joke the surprise ending of which has not been carefully prepared. But when the comic twist comes, like the
'twist' of enlightenment, it comes spontaneously and uncoerced. If it requires explanation and the effort of under-

standing it ceases to be funny, even when it is comprehended intellectually, and the attempt is made to force an embarrassed (but quite artificial) smile. If one does not get the point instantaneously and intuitively, laughter does not follow – i.e., it is not funny – though later one may come to understand the humour that was in it in a second-handed, discursive understanding.

The Explosion of Truth

Similarly, in the word tests of the disciple, or the verbal debates of the monks and masters, only the answer that is instantaneously, effortlessly and spontaneously given is acceptable, not the answer that follows the pause of reflection and reasoning, let alone a premeditated response, no matter how clever or ingenious it might be. Such could not represent a trans-rational insight or the intuitive perception of truth. A deliberated or rehearsed reply is evidence against rather than for the immediate plane of understanding that is here being solicited and tested. Realisation comes when it comes, and manifests itself when occasion demands, in a *ksana*' instant – *ksana*' being an expression for the smallest measure of time. It is the moment, that is to say, without temporal duration, the moment which immediately and spontaneously proceeds from the self-nature. As a moment it is qualitatively different from all other moments which seek to anticipate it or bring it into being. It is the Now in all its purity. One can prepare for it in a limited sense, as one sets the stage for the realisation of the point of a joke. But the preparation itself does not achieve the *ksana*' instant, which happens almost as if, like a comic perception and abrupt burst of laughter, it were unrelated or absurdly related to its preparation. Such a moment intersects time; it bursts into time; but it is not a continuation or elongation of the temporal process. It is not attached to the past or future; it is the moment which opens out into eternity.

This is not to negate the importance of careful preparation, whether through *zazen* meditational practice or the instruction of the master or the guidance of the sutras. Lu K'uan Yü argues that the *kōan*, for example, is properly used in relation to those disciples 'whose minds are already disentangled from illusions and whose potentialities are activated to the full, ready to absorb the truth.'[1] There is certainly a difference between a ripe and an unripe consciousness. And clearly the Zen masters, in using various techniques of indirect communication, presupposed some familiarity with the larger Buddhist tradition, and some inclination to move in the direction of its concerns and insights. They did not shout and laugh and kick in a vacuum. All effort and anticipation, however, involve the real danger of forfeiting the conclusion which, in a strict sense, does not follow from what has preceded it. If it were otherwise the perception would not be a new and revolutionary perception, but a continuation, however refined and perfected, of the old. Master Tai-chu (Daishu) put the matter very simply, quoting a sutra: 'The perception of Buddha-nature depends on the right moment, the direct cause [the seed of Buddhahood within], and the intervening cause [the precipitating occasion]. When the time is ripe, one is like a deluded man who is suddenly awakened and who has forgotten all about something which he suddenly remembers. Only then can his be the self-possessed (nature) which does not come from without.'[2]

Like comic appreciation, spiritual awakening has a *non sequitur* character about it. It comes spontaneously and uncoerced by anything that might attempt to give it birth. Hence both the Taoist and Zen emphasis upon no-effort and no-striving (*wu-wei*) which is easily confused with the counsels of a do-nothing party, or the advice of advocates of a cheap and easy enlightenment. Nan-chu'an (Nansen) was once asked by Chao-chou (Jyōshū), 'What is Tao?' 'Ordinary mind is Tao,' he replied. 'Should we try to get it?' Chao asked. 'As soon as you try you miss it.' 'How do we know without trying?' Chao pressed further. Nan-chu'an responded: 'Tao is beyond both knowing and not knowing. Knowing is false perception and not knowing is lack of awareness. When one attains to Tao it is certain that one will see it as clearly as one sees the vastness of the universe. Then what is the use of arguing about it?'[3]

The comic spirit, therefore, is not only analogous to, but akin to, the intuitive spirit that is central to Zen. In contradistinction to rationalism and empiricism, in both Zen and the comic sense there is involved an intuition which not only directly perceives the truth, and therefore dispenses with the construction of elaborate arguments and evidences which only postpone understanding indefinitely, but does so immediately. One either grasps the point instantly or not, which is something no amount of discussion of itself can effect. There is, of course, the case of the proverbial Englishman who gets the point of the joke and laughs a day later. Nevertheless, the delayed realisation of the joke comes, when it comes, abruptly and spontaneously. Explaining a joke, therefore, like explaining enlightenment, is the worst thing that could happen to it. For the rational translation of its non-rationality is totally different from getting the significance immediately and naturally – that is, from actually experiencing its humorousness. In the one case it is intellectualised, and though the point may be comprehended nobody laughs, indeed is prevented from laughing except in a nervous attempt at imitating the appropriate response. In the other case the laughter is not the result of purposively taking thought about the matter, and everybody laughs naturally and effortlessly.

The immersion in the immediacy of the moment in laughter is, thus, of the same order as the Zen emphasis upon entering and living within the Eternal Now. The moment of comic awareness is not a matter of reflection upon some process. There is no looking backward into the past or forward to the future, no retrospection or anticipation. Such a moment is free from the prisoning of analysis, and free from nostalgic attachment to the past or anxious attachment to the future. The moment which belongs to comedy and laughter is the present instant. To participate in comic insight is to participate in the immediacy and spontaneity of the Now. It is not an argument going somewhere or having been somewhere, but a procession brought to a sudden halt and plunged into the laughter of eternity.

It is for this reason that humour and Zen are so suited to each other, and in their spheres of coincidence so inseparable. Getting the point of a joke, or seeing things in comic perspective, like getting the 'point' of Zen, is something that cannot be reached either in strictly rationalist or empiricist terms, while smiling or laughing is a sign that one has moved beyond a mere discursive comprehension to a genuine understanding. Thus when Wēn Chēn-ching was asked, 'Who is the Buddha?' he laughed most heartily. The puzzled monk was taken aback: 'I do not see why my question makes you laugh so.' Wēn replied, 'I laugh at your attempt to get into the meaning by merely following the letter.'[4] Here the laughter of the master calls an abrupt halt to the false path being taken by the disciple, and invites him to a similar laughter with respect to the folly of his approach to the problem. If the point of the laughter is perceived, and if he too can begin to laugh, he will have already entered the true path.

This relationship was, in fact, suggested in the *Lankāvatāra Sūtra*: 'The discriminating-mind [*mano-vijñāna*] is a dancer and a magician with the objective world as his stage. Intuitive-mind [*manas*] is the wise jester who travels with the magician and reflects upon his emptiness and transiency.'[5] Herein is the clue to the jester-like triviality of so many *kōans* and *mondōs*, a triviality of the same sort as that in which comedy indulges. In answer to the classic Zen question as to the meaning of Bodhidharma's coming from the West, Fo-chien replied: 'When you taste vinegar you know it is sour, and when you taste salt you know it is salty;' San-shēng remarked, 'Tainted meat collects flies;' and Hsing-hua retorted, 'On the back of a broken-down donkey there are already enough flies!'[6]

Similarly the element of irrelevancy is another characteristic of the master's response to the monk's questions, a logical irrelevancy which points to the irrelevancy of reason in solving the problem – as in Ts'ao-shan's (Sōzan) response to the question, 'What is the nature of Buddha?' 'Three pounds of hemp!'[7] Like the comic employment of irrelevant speech or action, the whole scene is suddenly set in a radically different light. The normal train of thought and expectation is caught up short; it is interrupted and baffled; and one is forced to appropriate the situation in a very different manner. A jester's trick has been played on the discriminating mind (*mano-vijñāna*) by the intuitive-mind (*manas*), and consciousness is opened up to the moment in which a deeper awareness can break through.

The Comic Twist

A further correlation is also to be seen in the methodology of Zen 'midwifery' between the elements of suddenness, surprise and shock in the abrupt twist of humour and the similar virtues of the abrupt blow of the *keisaku*, as well as the slapping, kicking and shouting for which Zen masters have been notorious. These are all techniques of the same order and intent. Certainly in many cases such techniques may not be comic in any immediate sense, especially from the standpoint of the unenlightened disciple. Nothing is funny to him who fails to get the joke! Nonetheless, comic techniques and effects at least provide a helpful analogy in terms of which all such abrupt teaching (*tun-chiao*) methods and their desired results may be elucidated. Suddenness, surprise and shock are at the very heart of humour, and the stock-in-trade of the clown and comedian. Both the comic and the dramatic techniques (and, as has been argued, even the dramatic techniques have a comic dimension to them) are a form of spiritual 'shock therapy' which can serve to break up the patterns of thought and rationality that hold the individual in bondage. At a certain juncture further words and reasonings may only bind the cords more tightly, or perpetuate the illusion that the problem is solvable in these terms. What may be required, therefore, is the sudden jolt of the *kōan*, the irrational turn of the humorous anecdote, or the absurdity of the comic figure. If the individual has become removed from reality, if he has lost touch with the true nature of things, if he is caught in the web of artificial constructs, the function of humour, like that of the *keisaku*, can be that of snapping the bonds of his illusion, and bringing him back to reality.

The advantage and intent of such methods is summed up in Yüan-wu's (Engo) succinct comment on the *kōan* in the *Pi-yen-lu*: 'There is no crack in which to insert their intellectual teeth.'[8] Thus when Hsiang-yen's (Kyōgen) man, hanging precariously from a tree limb by his teeth, is called upon to 'Speak!' there is here no Kierkegaardian either/or which dramatically presents itself for some heroic ethical or religious decision, but a comic absurdity which thwarts any attempt at coming to terms with the situation through the ordinary channels of intellection and decision-making. Both alternatives are rendered impossible, forcing the resolution onto another plane. The choice however, between a more physical form of abruptness and surprise and a more humorous form – at least in the greater flexibility of the earlier Zen tradition – is a matter of accommodating the technique to the situation and individual involved. In full accord with the ancient practice among Indian and Asian spiritual masters of adjusting the approach to the specific personality and need of the individual, in some circumstances a more dramatic method might be required; in others a more comic method.

In either case, Zen is concerned with a different sort of knowledge and clarity than that of Descartes' 'clear and distinct ideas.' It is the clarity of *prajñā*, or direct, intuitive knowledge, in contradistinction to *vijñāna*, or discriminating, analytical knowledge. It is the clarity of the '*Kwatz*,' or of the clear and distinct blow on the head. It is the clarity of Chao-chou's (Jyōshū) 'Wu' (nothing) in response to the question, 'Has a dog a Buddha-nature or not?'[9] It is the clarity of that laughter which has perceived the element of comedy in any attempt to come to final terms with reality or with the self through ideas, however clear or distinct, or however fortified against doubt.

This is the thrust of the humorous title of Genrō's (18th century) collection of one hundred *kōans*: *Tetteki Tōsui*, or the *Solid Iron Flute Blown Upside Down*.[10] The caption itself indicates the folly in all claims to an intellectual attainment

of the wisdom toward which the *kōans* in the anthology point.
What could be more awkward and ridiculous, more clownishly
absurd, than the picture of a musician standing on his head,
attempting to play a tune by blowing on what turns out to be a
solid iron flute, his eyes bulging and his cheeks bursting in
dogged determination? And yet this, in the Zen view of it,
is a fitting symbol for the common folly of attempting to
'grasp' reality through the instruments of the discriminating-
mind. There must, therefore, be a frustration and confounding
of the intellect, so that its normal procedures will be checked
and its insistence on dominating the scene and calling all tunes
will be undercut. There must be an abdication of the lordship
of reason which assigns everything to its place in the abstract
system, saying to one 'go here' and to another 'go there.'
There must be a defeat of that rational imperialism which insists on possessing and governing all things as objects of its
thought, yet which ends up the prisoner of its own empire.
Proud reason must be made to appear in its comic patchwork
and motley colours, with the dialectician as dunce, and the
theoretician as dupe. The nimble wit, which has confidently
and yet anxiously leapt about, hardly touching the ground,
must be made to do what it will inevitably do: fall flat on its
face. There must be a collapse of some kind.

Hakuin's commentary on the *Hannya Shingyō*, which he
entitled *Dokugo* ('poisonous words of') *Hannya Shingyō*, is
illustrative of just such a collapse. The text is unusual indeed by
comparison with most commentaries on sacred scripture.
Under the pretence of praising and interpreting the sutra,
Hakuin in fact abuses and confuses it, advising the reader to, in
his words,

> *Throw this luxuriant entangling growth*
> *   That fills all the sky*
> *Over all the great monks of the Four Seas and Five Lakes,*
> *And tie them up.*[11]

The shock-value of this wry humour – on the surface blatantly
sacrilegious – is its own justification as a device for awakening

the reader to the pitfalls inherent in a mere intellectual and doctrinal acceptance of any religious teaching, however revered: that it may be substituted for the reality toward which it points, like 'mistaking the pointing finger for the moon.'[12] Or, as in the third case of the *Wu-mēn-kuan*, it may be a mistaking of the pointing finger of Zen for Zen. Chu-ti (Gutei), whenever asked a question about Zen would only reply by raising his finger. His attendant, therefore, when once asked about his master's doctrine, which he assumed to be admirably summed up in the master's gesture, aped his master in reply, and lifted a finger. When Chu-ti learned of this, he cut off the boy's finger. While the boy screamed in pain, Chu-ti again lifted his finger, and the boy was enlightened.[13]

Such was the insistence of the *Lankāvatāra Sūtra* itself, which says of its own doctrines: 'These teachings are only a finger pointing toward Noble Wisdom [*prajnā*] ... So with the teachings in all the sutras. They are intended for the consideration and guidance of the discriminating-minds [*mano-vijñāna*] of all people; but they are not the Truth itself, which can only be self-realised within one's deepest consciousness.'[14] So seriously are the warnings of this sutra taken that, from earliest times, as Lu K'uan Yü comments, 'Ch'an masters rarely used those Buddhist terms found in all sutras. For men are always prone to cling to the terminology which, in their quest for more learning and wider knowledge, can only stimulate their faculties of thought and intensify their discriminations.'[15] This, in Yün-mēn's (Ummon) blunter way of putting it would simply be to 'swallow the saliva of other people, and succeed in memorising and accumulating heaps and loads of curios and antiques.'[16]

In this lies the simple (yet by no means easy) realisation that the problem may be aggravated rather than resolved by any further pile-up of words and careful distinctions, however much Buddhist sutras indulge in them. It is better, in a sense, to be attached even to physical objects and sensuous delights than the often self-contained and self-perpetuating and in themselves completely unreal conceptualisations of the mind.

To circumvent this attachment and last retreat may require
some shocking and impious act, as in the case of Hsiang-yen
(Kyōgen) who, having studied his many sutras to no avail,
burned all his books and became a wandering monk, saying,
'A cake drawn on paper can never satisfy hunger.' Shortly
thereafter, as he was one day collecting grass at the ruins of a
monastery, he picked up a broken tile and tossed it away. It
struck a stalk of bamboo with a ping, and on hearing the sound
he was instantly awakened, and began laughing heartily.[17]

The Whole World taken by Surprise

The place of the comic in Zen may, thus, be viewed as parallel
to the two views of the place of painting in Zen: as a technique
for spiritual realisation, and as the expression of spiritual
realisation. It is not that the monk necessarily sees his situation
as particularly humorous initially, or that he is anticipating a
comic twist or collapse. Generally he is not; he is dead serious –
which, in fact, turns out to be part of the problem. He may
have sought enlightenment through scrutiny of the sutras,
pious acts, or long hours of meditation. He may have wrestled
in dialogue with the master. Or he may have attempted – with
intense concentration – to solve the insoluble *kōan* he has
been given. Perhaps he has been repeatedly rebuffed in *sanzen*
sessions with the master who has rejected his every solution.
The situation builds to a climax. The tension is seemingly unbearable. And a breaking point is reached. Then the release
comes, suddenly and simply. One escapes the vicious circle
of striving and grasping; and the tight hold of the ego and the
intellect is relaxed – often through the unexpected interven-
tion of an hilariously trivial and irrelevant event, like a tile
falling off the roof, or Bashō's frog jumping into the pond.
The absurdity of his former existence and effort, and the
absurdity of the precipitating occurrence, are suddenly revealed in the clear light of a new and revolutionary experience.
As K'ung-ku (Kukoku, 15th century) defined it, a *satori* is a
'grand overturning of the whole system of consciousness.'[18]
Or as Wu-mēn (Mumon) wrote concerning *satori* in his com-

mentary on the first case of the *Wu-mēn-kuan*: 'When the time comes for a final explosion, the result will resemble the whole world being taken by surprise.'[19]

Humour and laughter in Zen pedagogy, therefore – particularly relative to the psychology of the 'twice-born' – are not as extraneous as might appear at first hearing. For the elements of absurdity and surprise are the hallmarks of the comic twist and comic perception. Laughter is an explosive response to a situation which has suddenly been plunged into a contradiction or reduced to an absurdity. And yet out of that absurdity has come an unexpectedly different way of perceiving and responding to life. We commonly laugh in response to gaining some new insight into things, or solution to a perplexity, or resolution of a conflict. In laughter we reprimand ourselves with, 'Why didn't I think of that before?' Or we exclaim over our dullness in not having seen a truth that seems so simple and obvious and natural, a truth that has stood before us all the while, waiting for us merely to open our eyes to see it. We laugh at our former foolishness and blindness in the light of this new realisation, a laughter which also signifies our gratitude for the freedom from our former ignorance, and our enjoyment of the new being and new understanding that is ours. Hence, as R. H. Blyth also has suggested, 'enlightenment is frequently accompanied by laughing of a transcendental kind, which may further be described as a laughter of surprised approval.'[20]

An early Buddhist controversy arose over the question whether the Buddha, who had been credited by the sutras with having smiled on several occasions, smiled on seeing the subtle and sublime truth of enlightenment, or on seeing the foolishness and ludicrousness of the unenlightened. On the mutually accepted assumption that the source of smiling or laughter was the pleasurable, the issue was joined as to whether this pleasure in the case of the Buddha arose from observing the most exalted beauty and truth, or ugliness and error. It was Buddhadatta's thesis in the *Abhidhammāvatara* that the true source of the Buddha's smile was the degraded (*anulāra*) not the subtle (*anolārika*), though not necessarily in the Hobbesian sense of a feeling of 'glory arising from a sudden conception of some eminency in ourselves by comparison with the infirmity of others.' Rather, Buddhadatta argued, it was a smile in the sense of the Buddha's exultation over escaping the bonds of ignorance and desire, and a subsequent perception of their folly.[21] Yet this seems unnecessarily restrictive, for the source of such a smile may be just as much the sublimity and subtlety of the truth as the folly of the ignorance that preceded it. As in the case of the smile of Kāśyapa on the occasion of the Buddha's silently 'preaching' the sandalwood flower, this is the smile of a fresh realisation which brings with it both release and reintegration at a profounder level. In Blyth's words, 'laughter is a breaking through the intellectual barrier; at the moment of laughing something is understood; it needs no proof of itself.'[22] Such an interpretation embraces both *anulāra* and *anolārika*. Indeed, what finer source could laughter over foolishness have than a laughter from within the joy of some new-found, or re-found, insight?

It is out of such joy that even the most iconoclastic humour in Zen proceeds. Zen iconoclasm, for all its severity, conveys no animus or self-righteous indignation, but is grounded in the Bodhisattva ideal of enlightened compassion. However relentless its pursuit, or destructive its appearance, it is not motivated by dogmatism and intolerance, which would give it that arrogance and violence to which idol-smashing so easily falls prey. It is not an antagonistic humour with some hostile and aggressive intent, nor is it a self-enhancing stratagem for reinforcing one's own position and action, but the humour of compassionate love (*karunā*) and affection (*mettā*). If it laughs at ignorance and folly, if it debunks and ridicules and profanes, it does so out of the selfless wish to see others awakened and free.

There is, in fact, a certain lightness and liberty about this form of humour – sometimes giving to it an air of frivolity and sacrilege, because it does not seem serious enough. And it is not; for seriousness, too, is a cage of the spirit. Thus it is not born of an inner compulsion to strike out at others in some comic disguise, to convert others to one's own persuasion and in that way hopefully to fortify it, or to laugh other positions out of existence which threaten the position to which one is clinging. This is not the realm of anxiously attempting to prove something, to preach something, or protect something – of trying to 'make something out of it.' As Anagarika Govinda has phrased it: 'The Buddha's sense of humour – which is so evident in many of his discourses – is closely bound up with his sense of compassion: both are born from an understanding of greater connections, from an insight into the interrelatedness of all things and all living beings and the chain reactions of cause and effect. His smile is the expression of one who can see the "wondrous play of ignorance and knowledge" against its universal background and its deeper meaning. Only thus is it possible not to be overpowered by the misery of the world, or by our own sense of righteousness that judges and condemns what is not in accordance with our own understanding, and divides the world into good and bad. A man with a sense of humour cannot but be compassionate in his heart, because his sense of proportion allows him to see things in their proper perspective.'[23]

It is in this context and spirit that one may understand the unusual teaching of master Ch'in-niu (Kingyū, 8th century). Every day, it is reported, he would carry a cask of rice to the monks' quarters, crying out, 'Dinner is ready, O Bodhisattvas!' and then bellow with laughter. For twenty years, according to the Zen records, he taught in this fashion. In the words of Hsüeh-t'ou (Setchō):

> *Enveloped in masses of white clouds,*
> *Peals of loud laughter we hear,*
> *Something is being delivered to us*
> *From both his hands . . .*[24]

Ch'in-niu's laughter was not a laughter *at* his monks, nor even at their ignorance, or dullness, or folly. It was the compassionate, joyful laughter of him who has 'gone beyond', who

shows the way with a twinkle in his eyes, and who beckons all
to follow – into that region where only Spirit reigns, and the
Whole Truth may be told.

Notes

1. Luk, **I**, 11.
2. Luk, **II**, 58.
3. *Wu-mēn-kuan*, case 19; Ogata, page 108.
4. Suzuki, **III**, 105.
5. Goddard, page 70.
6. Suzuki, **II**, 223.
7. *Wu-mēn-kuan*, case 18.
8. Suzuki, **II**, 89.
9. *Wu-mēn-kuan*, case 1.
10. Senzaki and McCandless, translators, *The Iron Flute*.
11. Blyth, *Zen Classics*, **V**, 197.
12. A common Buddhist simile, and the title of a collection of Zen texts
    in 10 volumes, *Shigetsuroku*, 1602.
13. *Wu-mēn-kuan*, case 3.
14. Goddard, page 46.
15. Luk, **I**, 10.
16. Luk, **II**, 191.
17. Luk, **I**, 129.
18. Suzuki, **II**, 97.
19. *Ibid.*, page 252.
20. Blyth, *Oriental Humour*, page 89.
21. Shwe Zan Aung, page 26.
22. Blyth, *Oriental Humour*, page 91.
23. Govinda, page 177.
24. Suzuki, *Sengai*, page 9.

NINE *The Child of Tao*

> *Wise men hear and see*
> *As little children do.*
> LAO-TZU

> *If you wish to write haiku,*
> *Find a three-foot child.*
> BASHŌ

Before the aged Nan-chu'an (Nansen) passed away, his head monk asked him, 'Where are you going after your death?' The Master replied, 'I am going down the hill to be a water buffalo.' 'Would it be possible to follow you there?' inquired the monk. Nan-chu'an responded, 'If you want to follow me, please come with straw in your mouth!'[1]

As has been intimated throughout the foregoing, humour in Zen is not only, in a great variety of ways, an aspect of the method and technique of spiritual realisation. It is also the consequence and expression of this realisation. To see the world and one's individuality in this light is coincident with seeing it through the comic perspective, and *in* the comic spirit, at its profoundest level. To the degree that one is awakened, one is free to laugh in the deepest and most joyous sense – to laugh even in the face of the misfortunes of life and the inevitability of death. Herein lies the fullness of the comic vision.

> *Since my house burned down,*
> *I now have a better view*
> *Of the rising moon.*
> Masahide

Something of this spirit is captured in the account of the enlightenment of Shui-lao. Upon asking his master, Ma-tsu (Baso), 'What is the meaning of Bodhidharma's coming from the West?' Ma-tsu kicked him in the chest, knocking him to the ground. Immediately Shui-lao was awakened, got up, and began clapping his hands and laughing: 'How marvellous! How marvellous! Hundreds of thousands of *samadhis* and innumerable spiritual insights have their root in the tip of a feather!' Tai-hui (Daiye) reports that, when asked later about the nature of his enlightenment, Shui-lao replied, 'Since the master kicked me, I have not been able to stop laughing.'[2] Similarly, at the end of his life, Lo-shan (Razan, 9th century), sensing his end to be near, ascended the rostrum to speak. But instead of addressing his monks he abruptly dismissed them. He then remarked simply, 'If you wish to show your gratitude for the Buddha's goodness to you, you should not be too earnest about propagating the Great Teaching,' after which he began laughing loudly, and died.[3]

At every level of its manifestation, humour spells freedom in some sense and to some degree. Humour *means* freedom. This is one of its most distinctive characteristics and virtues. Here, however, the freedom to laugh which moves within the conflicts and doubts and tensions of life – the freedom, therefore, which is still relative to bondage and ignorance – becomes the freedom to laugh on the other side (the *inside*) of enlightenment. He who is no longer in bondage to desire, or to the self, or the law, he who is no longer torn apart by alienation and anxiety, and who is no longer defined and determined primarily by seriousness, can now laugh with the laughter of little children and great sages. Humour is caught up, and brought to fulfillment, in the joy of awakening and emancipation.

> *A tiny bubble of laughter,*
> *I am become the Sea of Mirth itself.*[4]

The End is the New Beginning

In Zen, as in any religious context, there are three levels on which the comic moves in relation to the sacred, three moments or moods which in mythological terms may be seen as corresponding to the laughter of Paradise, Paradise-lost and Paradise-regained. This is not intended to suggest any metaphysical commitment on the part of Zen teaching to such a mythological schema – e.g., the common mystical interpretation of the realm of *māyā* and *samsāra* as a 'fall' from some primordial oneness that is recollected in enlightenment and recovered in the achievement of *nirvāna*. In analysing the comic elements in Zen it is sufficient to understand the stages of this model as a movement from pre-rationality to rationality to 'supra'-rationality. Pre-rationality, then, represents the innocence and immediacy of infancy prior to the emergence of rationality, whose tendency is to split up the world into knower and known, subject and object, mind and body, good and evil, sacred and profane. While 'supra'-rationality represents the experience of transcending the dichotomies and estrangements of rationality in a recovery on a higher plane of that freedom and spontaneity and naturalness that is the special virtue of the child, and the symbolic achievement of the clown.

The place and function of humour in Zen may be interpreted as corresponding to these three levels. And at the same time Zen itself may be interpreted in terms of the place and function it gives to humour *vis-à-vis* any of these levels. What is of particular interest in Zen, however, and what has commanded the greater part of attention, is the way in which it approaches the matter of moving from the second to the third level of existence – a level which does not simply negate the other levels, but contains and embraces them (good-humouredly, in fact) on a profounder plane of being and knowing.

The use of such a mythological model is not arbitrary, nor simply a convenient methodological device. For, as I have argued elsewhere,[5] the various modes of the comic are precisely those that are symbolised in this mythical schema and the existential difficulties which it reflects: the playful return to childish innocence and impulse, an iconoclastic and often only cathartic response to present separations and anxieties, and the recovery of childlikeness in the epiphany of a new and redemptive resolution. At all three levels is to be found, in one form or other, what Joseph Campbell has called 'the gift of immaturity itself, which has enabled us to retain in our best, most human, moments the capacity for play . . . It is, in fact, only those who have failed, one way or another [to preserve this gift] in their manhood or womanhood, who become our penny-dreadfuls, our gorillas and baboons.'[6] Such 'immaturity' turns out to be the key to a genuine, rather than a pseudo-, maturity.

At the simplest level humour is a form of playing for the sake of playing. The clown cavorts, the comedian quips, the fool is foolish, and the spectator laughs out of sheer delight in the playfulness of the game of comedy itself. One is purposeless for the sake of being purposeless, nonsensical for the sake of being nonsensical, in but a simple and innocent refusal to make sense, or to be orderly, or to 'get serious' all the time. Here the comic spirit represents a leap into the playfulness of that 'wild and careless, inexhaustible joy of life invincible.'[7] It is not hostile or anxious or aggressive, but merely playful, intrigued and allured by awkwardness, absurdity and confusion. As such, humour is a movement back into the playful immediacy and spontaneity of childhood, the recovery (or attempted recovery) of the freedom and naturalness of innocent glee. It is the momentary, increasingly nostalgic, recapture of that world which is prior to the distinction between self and other, holy and unholy, cosmos and chaos, prior to the 'knowledge of good and evil' and the emergence of shame and guilt. It is, in short, the world that is symbolised by the mythical picture of a primeval Paradise, the 'Urzeit' that in Zen comes to be projected onto a higher plane as the 'Endzeit' of human experience.

Humour is not all innocence and play, however. At a more sophisticated and self-conscious level it stands more immediately within the sphere of duality, and in sensitivity to its conflicts and tensions, its alienations and anxieties. Here it is not a humour which leaves behind the world of dichotomy and rationality in a holiday of innocent abandon – a marvellously whimsical yet inherently unstable interlude – but is a humour which moves within the terms and delineations of the objectified self in comic response to them. It is, consequently, the comic mood as it corresponds to the fallen mythical state of Paradise-lost: the state of self-assertion, of desiring and grasping, of attachment and bondage, of separation and estrangement, of rational and moral discrimination. Instead of a recapitulation of the playful immediacy and spontaneity of the child, this level of humour is more self-conscious, more reflective, more serious, more mature. In fact, it shares in the same dualistic rifts in experience which elicit it and to which it is an inverted response. On the one hand it becomes an act of *withdrawal* from that which is ordinarily taken as serious and sacred (comic distance and detachment). And on the other hand it becomes an act of *aggression* against that which is ordinarily taken as serious and sacred (comic iconoclasm and profanation).

In this act of withdrawal or aggression is to be found a preliminary attempt at raising the matter to a higher plane, and at placing things in a larger perspective. The effort, however, often falls short either through affecting a pathetic leap backward into the irresponsible abandon of infancy, or through being satisfied merely with a temporary amelioration of the problem, and a momentary release of tension and conflict. Humour at this level does not, as it were, quite get off the ground, though a great deal of running to-and-fro takes place. It is not redemptive, but only cathartic. Or it gets off the ground self-deceptively by retreating to the first level of humour and burying its head periodically in the sands of a primordial innocence. It is simply regressive. Nevertheless, in the freedom of this half-playful, half-serious profaning of the ordinary world of perception, in its pitting chaos against cosmos, the profane against the sacred, or the irrational against the rational, lies the revelatory and redemptive potentiality of humour. A new order and a new being are heralded, however cryptically.

It is this world to which the clown and fool everywhere in their own inimitable, though ambiguous, way have called the spirit of man. Like the coxcombed clown of Europe in the middle ages, whose cock-feathers and cock-a-doodle-do could

be interpreted both as a reminiscence of the lost world of
animal impulse and the announcement of the dawn of a new
day of freedom, this holy foolishness recollects the world of
preconscious experience as a way of revealing the follies of
self-awareness, and of bringing into being the new dawn of a
fuller consciousness. The clown in his freedom stands outside
ordinary consciousness and beyond the confines of social conventions, sacred taboos, and rational enclosures. And the fool is
essentially beyond the law, whether the moral law or societal
law or the law of reason, which can mean not only prior to the
law, or over against the law, but actually *transcending* the law.
The clown and fool by occupying an ambiguous space between
the holy and the unholy, good and evil, wisdom and ignorance,
reason and nonsense, are particularly suited to this task of
pointing beyond all such distinctions, both backward to the
time before them and forward to the time that lies after them.
The clown's ability to garble all distinctions, and the fool's
inability to make the proper distinctions, prevision the sage's
capacity for moving beneath and beyond discrimination and
duality.

The position of *punctum indifferens* assumed by the clown-
fool, however, is a very difficult one to maintain, except as an
official stance. The 'point' is slippery. The tendency is to slide
off toward immorality or moralism, or to fortify the *status quo*
in the very act of providing temporary relief from it. Therefore any transcendence of the conflicts involved is often more
of a symbolic, than an actual, achievement. The spiritual
capacity to realise and sustain such a 'point' is usually not
within the character or power of the clown-fool as such. He
stands as a perennial reminder of it, a crooked pointing finger,
but not the whole 'point' itself. This is his role and his limita-
tion. Yet, for all his ambiguity and instability, he is the bearer
of a revelatory and redemptive possibility that, in Zen, is
appropriated as both a pedagogical method and psychological
mechanism for realising enlightenment and liberation.

In any event, to the degree that such an enlightenment and
liberation takes place, it then becomes possible to speak of a

third level of humour (and of the symbolism of the clown) in Zen: a comic spirit and perspective which, while it may include the former levels, is not identical with them, but decisively transcends them. Here humour becomes the freedom to laugh and to play which is contained within the freedom of enlightenment. Each level of humour implies and realises a certain type of freedom. But humour on this plane is distinguishable both from a nostalgic humour that proposes to return to the freedom of an early innocence and immediacy – which may only result in the euphoria of impulsiveness and insensitivity – and from an ambivalent humour that responds to the dichotomies and tensions of life in, at best, a cathartic attempt to cry out against them and relieve them. It is a humour that moves beyond the pitting of irrationality against rationality, beyond bondage to thwarted desire and threatened attachment, into the freedom of a higher innocence and immediacy. The playfulness of childlike spontaneity and naturalness has been recaptured and reaffirmed on a profounder level, a level which corresponds mythically to Paradise-regained. One has now become free, in the deepest and fullest sense, to laugh.

Beyond Good and Evil

In Taoism – undoubtedly influencing the early Ch'an masters – the schematisation of this realisation is that of seeing the form of the child as the model for the form of the sage. The sage does not return to childhood, *per se*, as if the sentimentality or senility of a second childhood were being recommended, but recovers *as a sage* the lost characteristics of childhood: purity, simplicity, unity, innocence, immediacy, spontaneity, naturalness, freedom.

For classical Taoism the principal ethical and religious question is that posed by Lao-tzu (6th century BC): 'Have you reached the state of a new-born babe?' The paradigm of a full humanity is to be found in the effortless and unitary spontaneity of the child, which is the nature of the Tao itself. To 'return again to infancy' is to 'return again to Primal Simplicity.' This is to be a true child of Tao. The sage, therefore, is one who 'desires to be desireless,' having the 'virtue of non-striving.' Thus, while 'all the people strain their ears and eyes, the sage only smiles like an amused infant.'[8] As Chuang-tzu rephrases Lao-tzu's position:

> *Can you be like an infant*
> *That cries all day*
> *Without getting a sore throat,*
> *Or clenches his fist all day*
> *Without getting a sore hand,*
> *Or gazes all day*
> *Without eyestrain?*
> *You want the first elements?*
> *The infant has them.*
> *Free from care, unaware of self,*
> *He acts without reflection.*[9]

This is not, however, simply a regression to infancy, as the passage seems to imply. When a disciple asks, 'Is this perfection?' Chuang-tzu has Lao-tzu respond:

> *Not at all.*
> *It is only the beginning;*
> *This melts the ice.*
> *This enables you to unlearn*
> *So that you can be led by Tao,*
> *Be a child of Tao.*[10]

According to Chuang-tzu, the Taoist master Nü-yü was once asked, 'Sir, you are advanced in years, and yet you still have the face of a child. What can be the secret?' Said Nü-yü, 'I have been instructed in Tao.'[11] To have drunk deeply of Tao, to have become a true child of Tao, is to have discovered, as it were, the fountain of eternal youth. This, in the teaching of the Sixth Patriarch, is a recovery of the Tao of one's 'original nature,' which is not to be understood as a return to a thought-less state. For such would render one 'equivalent to insentient beings, and would be a cause of hindrance in the Way.'

Rather, it is an achievement of attachment-less thought, for 'non-attachment is man's original nature' and 'that is freedom.'[12]

On this plane of non-attachment, the humour of the sage becomes the humour of an acceptance and celebration of the thusness and suchness of the world, transcending the anxiety over possessing and not-possessing, existing and not-existing, success and failure, the unrecoverable past and the unattainable future. The sage does not attempt to live in the abstract world of the desiring self, habitually refusing the reality of the immediate moment in favour of some bygone moment or anticipated moment or ideal moment – which would be a failure to really live at all. For the past, by definition, no longer exists; the future, as future, can never come; and the ideal, if actualised, could not be the ideal as such. The sage is one who, in the freedom of non-attachment and the immediacy of the present, is able to accept life and laugh at life, to receive life and to live life, completely in 'good humour' in spite of its tensions and contradictions. For he is no longer contained and trapped by the consequences of desire or a bondage to time. He has entered once again, in Yüan-wu's (Engo) terms, 'the *ksana*' instant in which "ordinary" and "holy" are transcended.'[13]

Though there is an apparent danger that this humour, and its acceptance and celebration of life, may sever the nerve of moral action and intellectual vision, it nevertheless represents a plane of transcendence apart from which one is hopelessly embroiled in the ultraseriousness of an insatiable striving, and in the futility of constantly emptying the present moment in favour of the unreality of past or future or ideal moments. As in the act of transcending the tensions between past and future, ideal and real, to transcend a bondage to such categories as good and evil, truth and error, meaning and absurdity, holiness and profanity, does not necessarily imply their complete revocation – which would indeed be regressive. Rather, the 'enlightened one' becomes a law unto himself. He is good in the goodness that lies beyond good and evil, and holy in the holiness that lies beyond sacred and profane – certainly the ideal of any ethic, whether of love or law. He does not seek to be good, or to be considered good, or to achieve the classification of saint or sage. Nor does he attempt to do the good on the basis of external criteria, rational persuasion, and a sense of obligation. He has recovered the freedom and spontaneity, the immediacy and unity, prefigured in both the child and the clown, of that spiritual maturity which rises above the artificiality of commandment and the tension between duty and desire. It is the inner freedom of naturally performing the good in the eternity of the Now.

In the words attributed to the Sixth Patriarch: 'For him who has once had an insight into his own Nature, no special posture as a form of meditation is to be recommended. Everything and anything is good to him, sitting, or lying, or standing. He enjoys perfect freedom of spirit, he moves along as he feels, and yet he does nothing wrong. He is always acting in accord with his Self-Nature. His work is play.'[14] Lin-chi (Rinzai), likewise, counsels his disciples: 'Followers of Tao, the way of Buddhism admits of no artificial effort. It only consists in doing the ordinary things without any fuss: going to the stool, making water, putting on clothes, taking a meal, sleeping when tired. Let the fools laugh at me. Only the wise know what I mean ... The truly noble man is a man of no concern and no ado. Don't try to be clever and ingenious. Just be ordinary.'[15]

This freedom from self and law is suggested in the more recent Zen favourite about Tanzan (1819–92) who was noted, among other things, for his lack of scrupulosity in keeping the Buddha's precepts with respect to sleeping, eating, drinking, etc. Though frequently looked upon with suspicion by those who had not gone very far beyond the level of 'washing the cup on the outside,' Tanzan nevertheless persisted in his freedom from bondage to the law. One of the Buddha's precepts, of course, has to do with the monks' relations to women. On one occasion Tanzan was travelling with another monk, Ekido, down a muddy road, where they met a beautiful girl in a fine silk kimono, unable to cross the intersection. Lifting her in his arms, Tanzan carried her across the road. Ekido did not speak to Tanzan until they reached a lodging temple that night, when he finally exploded angrily: 'Monks do not go near females, especially young and lovely ones!' 'I left the girl there at the crossroads,' replied Tanzan simply. 'Are you still carrying her?'[16]

Unfortunately, this freedom is sometimes confused with a shallow imitation of certain of the more bizarre, profane or incidental expressions of some of the great Zen masters, thus setting up a new orthodoxy of unorthodoxies – as if to behave strangely, or look peculiar, or become immoral or anti-intellectual is somehow a sign of authentic Zen and proof of spiritual maturity. It is like Lin-chi's monks who expended so much effort in imitating the master's renowned shouting thàt Lin-chi forbade any further shouting in the monastery until his disciples could first demonstrate their understanding of the meaning and proper moment for the shout, and even then not unless it became a natural and authentic expression of their own person and realisation. Yün-mēn (Ummon) was not so charitable about it: 'If you meet an old monk raising a finger or a dust-whisk [imitating the manner of certain masters] and saying, "This is Ch'an, this is Tao," you should raise your staff, give him a blow, break his head and then leave the place!'[17] But then Chu-ti (Gutei) was even less circumspect, summarily cutting off the finger of the attendant who copied his 'one-finger Zen' without having the corresponding spiritual attainment, leaving him with a 'no-finger' Zen!

The assumption seems to be that if one simulates certain of the incidental, or even substantive, consequences of enlightenment one becomes enlightened – which is like the man who leaps into the sea with the carefree abandon of the experienced swimmer, but who has not first learned how to swim. He drowns in his own pretensions! Greater than the problem of mimicry, however, is the confusion of spiritual freedom and spontaneity with a justification for some of the crassest forms of licence which, under the guise of liberation, become but another convenient excuse for doing as one pleases. Still less is this freedom in Zen to be confounded with giving free reign to certain infantile or animal impulses, and therefore presumably to the most 'natural' instincts. The problem is not one of the inhibition and repression of various elemental drives which must be released in order for the individual to be liberated. This would be a relapse of the lowest sort. Instead of making an advance on the situation, this only confuses impulsiveness for immediacy, indulgence for naturalness, and insensitivity for innocence. Under the mask of spirituality it is little more than a grand rationalisation for a retreat to some of the basest forms of ego, ignorance and desire. Like the nudist who imagines himself emancipated, but who has only become unbuttoned, such a misinterpretation of Zen freedom has mistaken a return to the irresponsible spontaneity of the child for a genuinely mature form of spontaneousness. Child-*likeness* is not to be equated with child*ishness*. The spiritual goal is not a giant step backward into a personal or primordial infancy, but the regeneration of one's Original Nature.

It is not that there is something so wrong about childhood, or in recovering moments of childish playfulness, as if one should forever be cut off from those moments which were once one's beginning and one's very life, or as if childhood were something to be despised. This is hardly the spirit which Pu-tai, spurning monastic life and playing and dancing and laughing with village children, symbolises. The adult who has forgotten what it means to be a child, who gives little evidence of ever having been a child, who is completely out of touch with his former self, is hardly the wiser or richer for it. He is aged perhaps, but not matured. In fact, for all the solemnity in his seriousness and no-nonsense, and for all his air of dignity and importance, he may be further from spiritual maturity than the childishness which he holds in contempt. From this standpoint, most of what passes for adulthood (spiritual or otherwise) is really only an extension of adolescence. It is none other than a prolongation of the adolescent attempt at demonstrating maturity by proving that one is no longer a child. The adolescent imagines that adulthood is achieved simply through a process of forgetting, repudiating and ultimately negating childhood. He has not yet discovered, in his loss of playfulness and in his newfound seriousness, that maturity is only reached by becoming once again like a little child.

In terms, then, of the mythological schema with which this essay began, the achievement of the comic spirit and perspective at its fullest in Zen may be interpreted as a corollary of the recovery on a higher level of that paradisal spontaneity, immediacy and naturalness enjoyed by the child – the freedom that is prior to the emergence of rationality and order, and the hiatus in experience between self and world, mind and body, good and evil, sacred and profane. Humour in Zen, therefore, at its profoundest, is more than a mere recapitulation of childish frivolity, and more also than a comic relief for tension and frustrated desire, or the comic reflection of anxiety, doubt and contradiction. And it is more than simply a Socratic and iconoclastic technique. In the freedom of enlightenment and liberation humour is transformed into the carefree laughter that transcends all those categories with which man would coerce the world, and which in turn make him a captive in his own prison. It has risen above both the ignorance that is innocence, and the ignorance that offers a knowledge of good and evil. It is the playfulness and lightheartedness that lies beyond his restless grasping and clinging, beyond the eternal torment of Tantalus, the sense of gaiety and festivity that lies on the further side of fear of death and attachment to the forms of life. One has learned what it means to become a child again, in the wisdom of the sage, the child of Tao.

The Laughter of Paradise-Regained

Most interpretations of humour recognise its existence on only two levels, corresponding mythically to the laughter of Paradise and Paradise-lost. And it is no doubt correct that most expressions of humour are instances of one or the other of these two types. Freud, for example, saw humour as essentially the endeavour to regain 'a pleasure which has really been lost in the development of (psychic) activity. For the euphoria which we are thus striving to obtain is nothing but the state of a bygone time, in which we were wont to defray our psychic work with slight expenditure. It is the state of our childhood in which we did not know the comic, were incapable of wit, and did not need humour to make us happy.'[18] The latter assertion needs some qualifications, since the child's first manifestation of its humanity is, in a sense, the smile of early infancy – hesitant and quivering at first, yet soon to be accompanied by laughter and the rudiments of a comic sense (in response to certain forms of suddenness, distortion and surprise). But, more importantly, this thesis gives to humour essentially a nostalgic movement of regression to the paradise of infancy, including the function of giving vent to impulses of hostility, aggression and desire which have been repressed and held in check by social restriction and inhibition (paradise-lost).

The same contention, of course, has been made with respect to religious experience: i.e., that it is a retrogression to a childish dependence upon some heavenly father-figure or, particularly in the case of mysticism, to the undifferentiated paradise of infancy and the womb. Though there is a modicum of truth in this, still in the most mature and therefore definitive realisations of both religious experience and the comic spirit, insofar as there is an element of recovery, it is a recovery of a qualitatively different sort. What is involved is a genuine transcendence and not simply a return or restoration, a transcendence which in one sense is a return and restoration – and to that extent the child is father of the man – but in decisively new terms and within a wholly new dimension. This achievement, to be sure, is in part grounded in and nurtured by 'recollection,' and in that special sensitivity nostalgic. But it is a distinctively new achievement. As such it is both identical with and radically other than this haunting paradise of remembrance. The experience that lies between the Alpha and the Omega of the spiritual pilgrimage is not simply a grand detour which counts for nought. Rather it is carried onto a higher plane of being and knowing; it is transcended and brought to fulfillment. In his *Iron Flute Blown Upside Down* Genrō captures this with characteristic wit:

> *The bellows blew high the flaming forge;*
> *The sword was hammered on the anvil.*
> *It was the same steel as in the beginning,*
> *But how different was its edge!*[19]

Erich Fromm has argued: 'Basically, there can only be two answers. One is to overcome separateness and find unity by *regression* to the state of unity which existed before awareness ever arose, that is, before man was born. The other answer is to be *fully born*, to develop one's awareness, one's reason, one's capacity to love, to such a point that one transcends one's own egocentric involvement, and arrives at a new harmony, at a new oneness with the world.'[20] If this latter 'overcoming' is not to be confused with the former (which is not really an overcoming at all), it is also not to be confused with a mediation of opposites through an uneasy compromise, like the precarious 'middle way' of the tightrope walker uncertainly suspended in mid-air. Such would be – though not regressive and escapist – only a repetition of the tensions and conflicts which it is claiming to have resolved. But here is a genuine *advance* upon these options and their 'solutions.' The humour which corresponds to this level, therefore, if not simply reducible to the laughter of the child, is also not reducible to what is, in effect, the laughter of adolescence, the laughter of Paradise-lost. It is the laughter of maturity, the laughter of Paradise-regained. It is the laughter of the *fully born*, to use Fromm's felicitous phrase – a phrase which is capable of including both the 'twice-born' emphasis of Rinzai and the 'once-born' emphasis of Sōtō.

Here there is no restless, anxious, striving humour in relation to the dramatic tensions of life, but an effortless, tranquil humour. It is the humour of *wu wei*, of harmonious rather than tense activity, which because of its spontaneity and effortlessness often appears to be the expression of naïveté or indifference or inaction. It is a humour which does not need to retreat into a holiday of childish innocence, for it has no need to escape. Nor must it withdraw into a comic distance to detach itself in order to achieve some momentary objectivity or relief. It is already detached (and therefore more powerfully involved) by reason of an inner non-attachment to self and to things. Nor does it need to be assertive or defiant, for there is no ego or grasping or possessiveness to be threatened and therefore protected. It is free to be the laughter of confidence and internal stability. It is not a nervous and insecure humour, seeking self-reinforcement and easily given to belligerence, but is the humour of an inward serenity, which therefore is capable of becoming, in the purest sense, the humour of compassion.

This is clearly the most dynamic and self-contained form of humour. For it does not derive its impulse from tension and anxiety, and therefore in large part from an outside source in relation to which it is dependent and determined – however well it may function as a mechanism for releasing pent-up energies, ameliorating conflicts, or redirecting animosities into less violent channels. It does not proceed out of a position of weakness, but of strength. Its power and stability arise from an inner harmony and assurance, and thus it moves with a force that flows from unity rather than opposition and strife. Grounded in *wu-shih* (no concern) and *wu-chi'in* (no seeking), it is the laughter of the highest freedom: freedom from all oppression of self and other, of desire and attachment, or of meaning and meaninglessness. Whether expressed in the serene smile of *sita* or the raucous laughter of *apahasita* and *atihasita*, it is a humour that lies beyond both seriousness and frivolity, sense and nonsense, purpose and purposelessness, in that joy which, as Chuang-tzu says, 'does all things without concern.'[21] It is the achievement of the comic spirit and perspective of one who has passed through Paradise-lost, who may have known alienation and anxiety, but who has come out on the other side that is identified in myth as Paradise-regained.

In this achievement is the solution to the touching nostalgia for the irretrievable paradise of Wordsworth's 'Recollections of Early Childhood':

> *Heaven lies about us in our infancy!*
> *Shades of the prison-house begin to close*
> *Upon the growing Boy . . .*
> *At length the Man perceives it die away,*
> *And fade into the light of common day.*

The world ruled by seriousness alone grows old, gnarled, sterile, wooden, rigid, lifeless. The grave world, indeed, is the world of the grave. But the world in the reign of the comic spirit grows young again – lively, vital, creative, dancing, joyful. It is a world that is not guarded, like Eden, by an angel with a flaming sword, but by Pu-tai and Ryōkwan, Han-shan and Shih-tē, and the laughing sages of Hu-hsi.

Three metamorphoses of the spirit do I designate to you: how the spirit becomes a camel, the camel a lion, and the lion at last a child.

Many heavy things are there for the spirit, the strong load-bearing spirit in which reverence dwells; for the heavy and the heaviest longs its strength . . . All these heaviest things the load-bearing spirit takes upon itself; and like the camel which, when laden, hastens into the wilderness, so hastens the spirit into its wilderness.

But in the loneliest wilderness happens the second metamorphosis: here the spirit becomes a lion. Freedom will it capture, and lordship in its own wilderness. Its last Lord it here seeks; hostile will it be to him, and to its last God. For victory will it struggle with the great dragon.

But tell me, my brethren, what the child can do, which even the lion could not do? Why has the preying lion still to become a child? Innocence is the child, and forgetfulness, a new beginning, a game, a self-rolling wheel, a first movement, a holy Yea.

Nietzsche, *Thus Spake Zarathustra*[22]

Notes

1. Chung-Yuan, *Original Teachings of Ch'an Buddhism*, page 163.
2. Wu, page 100; Blyth, *Oriental Humour*, page 90.
3. Blyth, *Zen Classics*, **II**, 33.
4. 'Samadhi,' Yogananda, page 154.
5. M. Conrad Hyers, ed., *Holy Laughter: Essays on Religion in the Comic Perspective* (New York: Seabury Press, 1969), ch. 13, 'The Dialectic of the Sacred and the Comic.'
6. *The Masks of God: Primitive Mythology* (New York: Viking Press, 1959), pages 39–40.
7. Joseph Campbell, *Hero With A Thousand Faces* (New York: Pantheon, 1949), page 28.
8. *Tao Teh Ching*, translated by John C. H. Wu (New York; St. John's University Press, 1961), x, 1; xxviii, 1; xxviii, 3; lxiv, 6; lxviii; xlix, 2.
9. Merton, xxiii, 7.
10. *Ibid.*
11. Wu, page 37.
12. Wing-Tsit Chan, translator, *The Platform Sutra* (New York: St. John's University Press, 1963), nos. 17–19, 14, 17.
13. *Pi-yen-lu*, case 46; Shaw, page 158.
14. Suzuki, **I**, 217.
15. Wu, page 203.
16. Reps and Senzaki, page 18.
17. Luk, **II**, 196.
18. Sigmund Freud, *Wit and Its Relation to the Unconscious*, translated and edited by A. A. Brill, *The Basic Writings of Sigmund Freud* (New York: Modern Library, 1938), page 803.
19. Senzaki and McCandless, page 29.
20. *Zen Buddhism and Psychoanalysis* (New York: Grove Press, 1963), page 87.
21. Merton, xii, 1.
22. Friedrich Nietzche, *Thus Spake Zarathustra*, translated by Thomas Common (New York: Random House, n. d.), pages 23–5.

Epilogue

A contemporary Ch'an master, Hsüan Hua, thus concluded his talk at the end of a *sesshin*, or week of intensive meditation:

> Now we have finished. Everyone stand and we will bow to the Buddha three times to thank him. We thank him, because even if we did not have a great enlightenment, we had a small enlightenment. If we did not have a small enlightenment, at least we didn't get sick. If we got sick, at least we didn't die. So let's thank the Buddha.[1]

Note
1. *Vajra Bodhi Sea*, **I**, 3 (October, 1970), page 40.

Index